A RENTER'S JOURNEY

Introduction

Introduction

Welcome, renters and those about to step into the exciting world of leasing! In this guide, "A Renter's Journey," we'll embark together on a path that demystifies the often perplexing terrain of renting. It's my privilege to serve as your guide, bringing to the table insights from my previous work, "YOU TOO! CAN MAKE MONEY IN RENTAL PROPERTIES." While my earlier endeavors focused on the property owner's perspective, I've shifted gears to empower you, the renter, with the knowledge and tools necessary for making informed decisions in the rental market.

I'm L.T. Judd, and my transition from advising property investors to assisting renters was motivated by a simple truth: everyone deserves a fair shot at finding their ideal home. This book is my way of ensuring you have that shot, equipped with an understanding of your legal rights, the ins and outs of negotiation, and how to weigh the cost against the quality of management.

Our target audience is adult renters at any stage of their journey. Whether you're signing your first lease or a seasoned tenant searching for a better deal, this guide is crafted with you in mind. "A Renter's Journey" is not just about finding a place with the right rent; it's about understanding the broader picture, including your rights and how to foster a positive relationship with landlords.

The title, "A Renter's Journey," encapsulates our comprehensive coverage, from legal assistance and financial strategies to personal anecdotes and real-world concerns. This book stands out by combining essential knowledge with practical exercises, making the renting process less intimidating and more accessible.

Acknowledging the challenges and fears often accompanying the renting process, I promise to offer sympathy and solutions. Through actionable advice and insider tips, we'll tackle these challenges head-on, ensuring you're prepared to confidently navigate the market. Structured to build your knowledge step by step, this book guides you through the various aspects of renting, ensuring no stone is left unturned. From understanding your lease to negotiating confidently, we've got you covered. Let me leave you with a thought that drove much of my work: "Knowledge is power, especially when finding your next home." This mantra underscores the importance of being well-informed in your renting decisions. So, I invite you to join me on this enlightening journey. Together, we'll explore every facet of the rental process, turning complex legal jargon and daunting negotiations into manageable tasks. Consider this book not just a guide but a companion on your quest for a place to call home. Let's get started.

Contents

Chapter 1

♥

The Journey

Stepping into the world of renting can feel akin to navigating a dense forest without a map. One of renters' first and most significant challenges is understanding the lease agreement. This document, often laden with legal terminology and fine print, is the bedrock of the tenant–landlord relationship. It's where expectations are set, responsibilities are outlined, and the rules of engagement are established. Given its importance, one might expect a lease to be straightforward to understand, yet many find themselves needing clarification , wondering if they've missed something crucial amidst the jargon.

1.1 The Anatomy of a Lease Agreement

Understanding Lease Structure

A lease agreement is not just a piece of paper; it's a binding contract that outlines the terms under which you're allowed to occupy a property. Think of it as a rulebook for your tenancy. Typically, these agreements follow a structured format, beginning with identification details for the tenant and the landlord, followed by a rental property description. This introduction sets the stage, ensuring all parties are identified and the agreement's subject is unmistakable.

Identifying Key Components

Within the body of the lease, several vital components demand your attention. The term length specifies how long you have rights to occupy the property, be it a year, month-to-month, or another arrangement. This section anchors your tenancy, giving you a timeline for your stay. Next, the rent amount section details how much you'll pay and when and how these payments should be made. Misunderstanding this segment can lead to late fees or, in worse cases, eviction. The security deposit details, often a source of confusion and conflict, clarify what is expected upfront to cover potential damages and under what conditions you can expect this amount to be returned. These components form the financial backbone of your agreement, outlining your immediate fiscal responsibilities.

The Importance of Clauses

Delving deeper, you'll encounter various clauses that dictate how the property can be used, restrictions on behavior, and the consequences of violating these terms. For example, a pet clause will clearly state whether pets are allowed and under what conditions, potentially including restrictions on size, breed, or number of pets. Similarly, a subletting clause determines whether you can rent the property to someone else, a crucial consideration if your plans change. The landlord's expectations are explicitly stated in these clauses , and understanding them is critical to maintaining a good relationship with your landlord and avoiding penalties.

Spotting Omissions

Notably, what a lease doesn't say can be as important as what it does. Without clear maintenance and repair responsibilities, you might be uncertain about who to call when the sink leaks. A missing clause on the lease renewal process could have you scrambling at the end of your lease term, unsure of how to proceed. These omissions can create confusion, leading to misunderstandings or disagreements. In these cases, tenants often find themselves at a disadvantage, faced with unexpected responsibilities or needing protections they assumed were in place. In every section and clause of a lease, there lies an opportunity to ensure your rights are protected, and your responsibilities are clear. This document, while daunting at first glance, is your best defense against potential disputes and misunderstandings. As you navigate through its terms, remember that knowledge is your ally. With a thorough understanding of your lease agreement, you'll be well-equipped to create a harmonious living situation where surprises are few and your stay is enjoyable.

1.2 Common Lease Clauses and What They Mean

Rent and payment clauses, maintenance and repair responsibilities, subletting and assignment clauses, and termination and renewal terms are the backbone of most lease agreements. Each section carries its weight in defining the tenant-landlord relationship, and understanding them can significantly impact your renting experience.

Rent and Payment Clauses

Rent is more than just the monthly amount you pay to live in your rental; it's a detailed agreement covering how payments should be made, when they are due and what happens if they're late. Typically, this clause will specify: Payment Methods : Whether payments can be made online, by check, or through direct deposit. Some landlords may prefer one method over another, and knowing this upfront is crucial to avoid complications.

Due Dates and Grace Periods

While rent is commonly due on the first of the month, landlords may offer a grace period, a short span where late fees aren't applied, typically four days, or due no later than the 5th of the month. Knowing this period can offer a buffer in tight financial months.

Late Fees

The specifics about late fees, including the amount and when they start accruing, are critical. These fees can add up quickly, making a late rent payment significantly more expensive. Some states limit how much a landlord can charge on the first day the rent is late and then per day after that, so it is a good idea to go online and find out if your state has any limitations.

Maintenance and Repair Responsibilities

Clarity on who handles various maintenance tasks and repairs ensures a well-maintained living space and can prevent disputes. This clause often divides responsibilities as follows:

Landlord's Responsibilities

Generally, the landlord is responsible for ensuring the property remains habitable. This includes significant repairs and maintenance tasks such as fixing heating and plumbing issues, providing the building's structural integrity, and addressing mold or pest infestations.

Tenant's Responsibilities

Tenants typically handle minor maintenance and upkeep, like changing light bulbs, keeping the property clean, and minor repairs, such as unclogging drains if caused by the tenant's misuse. It's common for tenants to be responsible for the damage they or their guests cause.

Subletting and Assignment Clauses

Subletting can offer flexibility if you need to leave your rental for a period but plan to return. However, not all leases allow it. This clause provides details on:

Permission to Sublet

Some leases require the tenant to obtain written permission from the landlord before subletting. This section should outline the process for seeking approval.

Subtenant Approval

Landlords may reserve the right to approve any subtenants based on their standard rental criteria.

Responsibility for Rent

Even if you sublet your rental, you remain responsible for ensuring the rent is paid and the property is well cared for. Understanding your obligations and the potential consequences of your subtenant's actions is vital.

Termination and Renewal Terms

Knowing when and how your lease concludes is as essential as knowing what it entails during your stay.

These terms cover Lease Duration

Whether your lease is fixed-term (e.g., one year) or month-to-month affects how you and your landlord can terminate the agreement.

Renewal Options

Some leases automatically renew unless the tenant or landlord provides notice of intention not to renew within a specific timeframe. Others may require active renewal, where both parties must agree to extend the lease.

Notice Requirements

This specifies how much notice you must give if you decide to move out, typically 30 or 60 days before the lease ends. Similarly, it outlines how much notice your landlord must provide if they choose not to renew the lease or if they need to terminate it early for reasons outlined in the agreement.

Early Termination

In some cases, leases include conditions under which either party can terminate the agreement early, such as a job relocation. Penalties or fees for early termination should also be clearly stated. Each of these clauses is crucial in defining your rights and responsibilities as a tenant. They set clear expectations for both parties and provide a framework for addressing any issues that may arise during your tenancy. Understanding them helps build a solid foundation for a positive renting experience, ensuring you know what you're agreeing to before you sign and what steps you can take if something doesn't go according to plan.

1.3 Red Flags in Lease Agreements

You Shouldn't Ignore

Navigating a lease agreement might encounter terms that raise eyebrows or cause hesitation. Paying attention to these signals is vital, as they can lead to discomfort or financial strain during your tenancy. Here, we discuss several red flags that warrant a second look or, at times, may require some negotiations or even suggest looking for a different property altogether.

Excessive Fees and Penalties

While it's reasonable for landlords to include fees and penalties to ensure tenants adhere to the lease terms, there's a fine line between fair compensation and exploitation. High fees for minor infractions or hefty penalties for breaking the lease early can signify that the landlord prioritizes profit over tenant welfare. Moreover, a long list of potential fees for various scenarios could indicate an approach that seeks to nickel-and-dime tenants at every turn. This situation puts a financial strain on renters and can create a tense atmosphere where one is constantly wary of incurring additional costs.

Vague Maintenance Clauses

A well-defined maintenance clause is crucial for a hassle-free living experience. It should delineate which responsibilities fall to the tenant and which are the landlord's. Ambiguities in this area can lead to disputes and out-of-pocket repair expenses that should not be the tenant's burden. For instance, if a lease vaguely states that tenants are responsible for "keeping the property in good condition," this could mean anything from regular cleaning to significant repairs. Such vagueness can also leave tenants vulnerable to landlords who may shirk their responsibilities, leaving renters to deal with malfunctioning appliances or deteriorating building conditions.

Restrictive Guest Policies

While landlords have the right to implement policies that protect their property and the peace of the community, overly restrictive guest policies can infringe on your right to use and enjoy your rental. Restrictions that limit the number of guests you can have, how long they can stay, or require guest registration might seem excessive. They could indicate a landlord's desire for control beyond reasonable property management. These policies could also complicate your social life and personal relationships, making it challenging to host gatherings or have long-term visitors like family members.

Lack of Recourse for Breach of

"Quiet Enjoyment"

"Quiet enjoyment" refers to a tenant's right to use their rental without unreasonable disturbance from landlords, their agents, or other tenants. This includes freedom from excessive noise, disruptions from ongoing construction, and other nuisances. A lease that lacks mention of recourse or remedies for violations of quiet enjoyment might signal that the landlord does not prioritize tenant comfort or has yet to consider how to handle such issues. Without clear guidelines or avenues for addressing disturbances, tenants may endure ongoing noise or disruptions with no clear way to request intervention or compensation.

These red flags do more than merely hint at potential issues; they spotlight aspects of the leasing and living experience that could significantly impact your satisfaction and comfort. When reviewing a lease, it's crucial to approach these red flags not as mere hurdles but as opportunities to engage in open dialogue with potential landlords. Asking for clarification, seeking adjustments, or deciding that a particular lease isn't for you are all valid responses prioritizing your needs and well-being as a renter.

1.4 Negotiating Your Lease:

Yes, It's Possible!

The excitement is palpable when you find a place that feels like it could be your next home. However, before you let that excitement carry you away, remember that the lease agreement before you aren't set in stone. Many renters need to realize there's room for negotiation in lease terms, which can lead to more favorable living conditions and even financial savings.

The Power of Negotiation

The notion that lease terms are rigid is a common misconception. Landlords are often open to negotiations, especially when securing a responsible tenant for their property. The key to successful negotiation is understanding that it's a two-way street; you and the landlord have goals you wish to achieve. Presenting your requests as mutually beneficial increases the likelihood of a favorable response. For example, if you're looking to secure a lower rent, consider offering a longer lease term in return, which guarantees income stability for the landlord.

Strategies for Successful Negotiation

Approaching lease negotiation with confidence is crucial. Here are some practical tips to prepare you for a successful negotiation. Do Your Homework! To understand average rents for similar properties, research the local rental market . This information gives you a solid foundation to argue for fair pricing based on market rates.

Highlight Your Strengths as a Tenant

Prepare to showcase your reliability. This can include a steady income, a good credit score, positive references from previous landlords, or a history of long-term tenancies. Be clear and concise in your requests. When you know what changes you want in the lease agreement, articulate them clearly. Whether it's a rent reduction, permission to have pets, or a different lease term, being specific helps avoid misunderstandings.

Listen to the Landlord's Perspective

Understanding the landlord's priorities can help you tailor your requests. If they're concerned about property maintenance, offer to take on minor upkeep tasks in exchange for lower rent or other concessions.

Common Negotiable Lease Terms

Knowing which aspects of a lease are typically more flexible can guide your negotiation efforts. Commonly negotiable terms include rent amount. Landlords might be willing to adjust the rent to secure a tenant, especially in markets with high vacancy rates.

Lease Duration

Landlords prefer not to have vacant properties. Offering to sign a longer lease might incentivize them to provide better terms.

Security Deposit

While state laws might regulate the amount, there's often room to negotiate the payment terms, such as paying installments.

Renewal Options

You might negotiate terms under which the lease can be renewed, including caps on potential rent increases.

Pet Policies

If the initial lease prohibits pets or includes a pet deposit, these terms can often be negotiated, significantly if you can demonstrate responsible pet ownership.

What to Do If Negotiations Stall

Even with the best preparation, negotiation is only guaranteed to achieve the desired outcome. If you find that negotiations are stalling, consider these steps, take a Break. Sometimes, stepping away for a few days can give both parties the space to reconsider their positions. A brief pause can lead to more flexibility in subsequent discussions. Reassess your requests, considering the market and the property, are your negotiation points reasonable. Adjusting your demands might help move things forward.

Seek Compromise

If specific terms are non-negotiable for the landlord, see if there are other areas where they might be more flexible. For instance, if a rent reduction isn't possible, a parking space could be included at no extra cost. Be prepared to walk away If the lease terms don't meet your needs and the landlord isn't willing to budge, it might not be the right fit. Remember, finding a comfortable home where you feel valued as a tenant is essential. Negotiating a lease requires a delicate balance between assertiveness and flexibility. By entering negotiations well-prepared and clearly understanding your objectives and the landlord's, you can confidently navigate these discussions. While not every negotiation will not result in any changes to a lease agreement, even small concessions can make a significant difference in your living situation. Remember, landlords value reliable, responsible tenants, and if you can demonstrate your value, you might be surprised at the willingness to accommodate your needs.

In the realm of renting, knowledge truly is power. Understanding the potential for negotiation and approaching it with the right strategies can transform your lease agreement from a set of rigid terms to a flexible foundation for your tenancy. With these insights on negotiating your lease, you're better equipped to secure a rental agreement that aligns with your needs, setting the stage for a satisfactory and enjoyable renting experience.

1.5 Legal Jargon Simplified:

Lease Language You Need to Know

In the realm of lease agreements, the devil often lurks in the details, hidden within the legal jargon that sometimes sounds like a foreign language. Tenants must cut through this complexity, transforming these terms into explicit, actionable knowledge. This section aims to demystify legal terminology, spotlight critical phrases, and illustrate how the language of your lease impacts your tenant rights. Additionally, we'll guide where to turn for further clarification, ensuring you're fully equipped to navigate the legal landscape of your lease.

Deciphering Legal Terminology

At their core, lease agreements are legal documents, and as such, they're peppered with terms with specific legal implications. Understanding these terms clarifies your obligations and rights and empowers you to advocate for yourself more effectively. Here are a few standard terms you might encounter.

Lessee and Lessor

These formal terms refer to the tenant and landlord, respectively.

Premises

This term denotes the rental property. It's essential to ensure the description matches the property you've agreed to rent, including any specific units or parking spaces.

Covenant

A covenant in a lease is a promise in a legal sense. For instance, a "covenant of quiet enjoyment" assures the tenant a peaceful occupancy without disturbance from the landlord beyond what's reasonable.

Subrogation

This legal principle allows an insurer to pursue a third party that caused an insurance loss to the insured. It's often mentioned in contexts where renters' insurance is required, outlining the rights of insurance companies in the event of a claim.

Key Phrases and Their Implications

Lease documents are also home to phrases that may seem innocuous and carry significant weight. Recognizing these phrases and their implications is critical to understanding the broader context of your rights and responsibilities.

Wear and Tear

This phrase acknowledges that some deterioration is expected over time due to everyday use. It's significant because it delineates what kind of damage a tenant won't be financially responsible for at the end of a lease.

Right of Entry

While landlords have the right to enter the rental property for specific reasons, such as emergency repairs or inspections, this phrase should be accompanied by conditions that respect your privacy, like advance notice and reasonable hours.

Renewal Option

This phrase indicates whether you can renew your lease and under what terms, a crucial detail as your lease end approaches.

Understanding Your Rights Through Language

The specific wording of your lease can significantly impact your rights as a tenant. For instance, a lease stipulating the landlord may enter at any time for any reason infringes on your right to privacy and quiet enjoyment. Conversely, a lease that outlines specific, reasonable conditions for entry, such as providing 24-hour notice for non-emergency inspections, protects those rights. Similarly, clauses related to rent increases, lease renewals, and termination notices should be scrutinized for fairness and legality. Understanding the implications of these terms ensures you're entering into an agreement that respects your rights and sets clear expectations for both parties.

Resources for Further Clarification

Navigating the complexities of lease agreements doesn't have to be a solo venture. Various resources are available to help you further clarify the legalities of your lease.

Tenant Rights Organizations

Local and national organizations offer resources, counseling, and sometimes legal representation for tenants seeking to understand their lease agreements better.

Legal Aid Services

For those who might not have the means to hire a private attorney, legal aid services provide free or low-cost legal assistance, including help with leases.

Online Legal Services

Platforms like NOLO and LegalZoom offer guides and articles on standard lease terms and tenant rights. Some also provide access to legal documents and even consultations with attorneys for a fee.

State and Local Housing Authorities

Government agencies often publish tenant guides that explain lease terms and tenant rights in simple language tailored to the specific laws of your state or city. Remember that knowledge is your greatest ally when wrapping up this exploration of lease language and legal jargon. By breaking down complex terms into understandable concepts, you equip yourself with the ability to navigate your lease agreement confidently. This understanding clarifies your obligations and rights and empowers you to spot potential issues and seek adjustments where necessary. With these tools, you're well-prepared to ensure your lease serves your interests and supports a positive, fair rental experience.

1.6 Renewing Your Lease: What to Consider Before Signing Again

The moment you find yourself nearing the end of your lease, a decision looms on the horizon: to renew or not to renew. This choice, while seemingly straightforward, involves carefully evaluating your current living situation, the terms on offer for renewal, and how both align with your plans and references.

Evaluating Your Current Situation

First, take stock of how well your rental has served you. Reflect on the location, size, amenities, and whether these still match your needs. For some, changes in job location, family size, or even lifestyle might shift what's essential in a home. Beyond the physical space, consider your relationship with the landlord and neighbors. A harmonious living environment can be just as crucial as the apartment's features.

In assessing your situation, think about:

Changes in your commute or job location that might make another area more appealing. Any growing space needs, perhaps due to working from home or changes in family size. The overall satisfaction with how property management addresses maintenance requests and other concerns.

Negotiating Lease Renewal Terms

If the scales tip towards staying, entering renewal negotiations informed and prepared can lead to more favorable terms. Remember, landlords value reliable tenants and might be open to negotiations to avoid vacancy costs.

For a successful negotiation:

Research the current rental market to understand if you can ask for better terms due to decreased market rates or high demand in your area. Consider what you're willing to offer in return, like a longer commitment, which can be attractive to landlords looking for stability. Be clear about what changes or improvements would enhance your continued tenancy, whether it's apartment updates or lease terms like pet policies or amenities. During these discussions, focus on creating a win-win situation. Highlight your timely rent payments and care for the property as reasons you're a tenant worth keeping on favorable terms.

Pros and Cons of Lease Renewal

Renewing your lease can offer several benefits, including avoiding the hassle, time, and expense involved in moving. Staying put means no packing, searching for a new place, or adapting to a new neighborhood. Additionally, if you've negotiated effectively, you might secure a better deal or necessary improvements to your rental. On the flip side, renewing your lease might mean taking advantage of opportunities that better align with your evolving needs or financial situation. The rental market might offer more competitive rates or enticing living situations elsewhere. Moreover, if unresolved issues exist with your current rental or landlord, renewing could mean another year of dealing with the same frustrations.

When to Walk Away

Deciding not to renew your lease is a significant decision that should be made with both your head and heart. It might be time to start looking for a new place if your needs have outgrown the space, and compromises on your lifestyle or work situation are no longer viable. Consistent issues with maintenance or management have affected your quality of life, and there's little indication of improvement. Financial considerations, such as a rent increase not matched by upgrades or improvements to the property, make staying less appealing. Exploring a new neighborhood or city aligns more closely with personal or professional growth opportunities. In making this decision, weigh the tangible costs of moving against the intangible benefits of a living situation that better fits your current life phase. While moving can be daunting, it also opens the door to new possibilities and environments that could offer a more fulfilling living experience. In contemplating lease renewal, the process requires a mix of introspection about your current satisfaction and future needs, strategic negotiation to secure terms that reflect your value as a tenant, and a clear-eyed assessment of the benefits and drawbacks of staying put versus moving on. Each step in this process is essential, guiding you towards a decision that makes sense from a practical standpoint and aligns with your aspirations and lifestyle goals.

1.7 Breaking a Lease:

Legalities and Etiquette

Life is full of unexpected twists and turns, and sometimes, these unforeseen circumstances can lead to a situation where you need to break a lease agreement early. While approaching this topic can be daunting, understanding your rights, the potential consequences, and strategies for minimizing the impact can help navigate this complex process with respect.

Understanding the Consequences

When you sign a lease, you enter into a binding legal agreement to rent a property for a specified period. Breaking this agreement early can lead to several consequences, both legal and financial. Legally, landlords may have the right to pursue damages in court, leading to potential legal fees on top of any owed rent. Financially, tenants might be responsible for rent payments until the end of the lease term or until the unit is re-rented, in addition to potential fees outlined in the lease for early termination. These repercussions underscore the importance of proceeding with caution and informed awareness.

Legitimate Reasons for Early Termination

While breaking a lease can come with penalties, there are several circumstances under which you might legally terminate a lease early without facing these consequences. These include military deployment. Federal law allows service members to break their leases under specific conditions related to deployment or permanent change of station.

Domestic Violence

Many states provide legal protections that allow victims of domestic violence to terminate a lease early for their safety. Habitability Issues, If a landlord fails to maintain the property livable, tenants may have a right to break their lease.

Violation of Privacy

Repeated, unjustified intrusions by a landlord can sometimes justify lease termination. These scenarios are recognized by many state laws as valid reasons to end a lease early, underscoring the importance of familiarizing yourself with local tenant laws.

How to Approach Your Landlord

Communication is the key to addressing the need to break a lease with your landlord. Here are steps to ensure the conversation goes as smoothly as possible.

Early Notification

Inform your landlord as soon as you know you must leave. This courtesy can make a significant difference in how they respond.

Written Notice

Follow up your conversation with a formal, written notice detailing your departure date and its reasons, providing documentation if necessary.

Honesty and Transparency

Be open about your reasons for leaving. Your landlord might be more understanding if it's due to a job relocation, health issues, or another significant life change.

Propose Solutions

Whether helping to find a new tenant or offering to pay a portion of the remaining rent, proposing solutions can make the process easier for both parties. Taking a respectful, proactive approach can

go a long way in maintaining a positive relationship with your
landlord during this transition.

Mitigating Financial Impact

Minimizing the financial repercussions of breaking a lease requires a strategic approach. Here are some strategies that might
help:

Subletting

If your lease and state laws allow, finding someone to sublet your
apartment can cover the rent for the remainder of your lease term.

Lease Takeover

Similar to subletting, a lease takeover involves finding someone to assume your lease, effectively releasing you from your
obligations. This option is often more appealing to landlords as
it provides a more stable solution.

Negotiate an Early Termination Fee

Some landlords might be willing to accept an early termination
fee instead of rent for the remaining months. This fee is typically
less than what you would owe for the duration of the lease and
can be a viable option for both parties.

Utilize Legal Protections

If you're breaking your lease for one of the legally recognized reasons mentioned earlier, ensure you're fully aware of your rights and the proper procedure to minimize or eliminate financial penalties. These strategies, while only sometimes guaranteed to work, provide a starting point for those needing to exit a lease early. They underscore the importance of understanding your lease, maintaining open lines of communication with your landlord, and being aware of the legal landscape that governs tenant rights in your area. Breaking a lease early is a decision that comes with significant considerations. You can navigate this process more effectively by understanding the potential consequences, knowing the legitimate reasons for early termination, carefully approaching your landlord, and employing strategies to reduce the financial impact. Remember, while breaking a lease is far from ideal, life's unpredictable nature sometimes makes it necessary. Approaching the situation with respect, preparation, and a clear understanding of your rights can help make this transition as smooth as possible, preserving your financial well-being and rental history.

1.8 Lease Addendums:

Adapting Your Lease to Life Changes

Life rarely follows a predictable script, and changes can prompt a need to modify your living arrangements. You and your landlord can update the lease agreement through an addendum when these shifts occur . This document becomes part of the original lease, adapting it to new circumstances without drafting a completely new agreement.

Purpose of Addendums

Addendums serve to modify, clarify, or nullify terms in the existing lease without voiding the entire contract. They're handy for incorporating terms that were not initially anticipated. For instance, obtaining a new pet, changing roommates, or altering payment terms due to unforeseen financial hardships typically necessitate an addendum. This flexibility is invaluable, as it allows both tenant and landlord to adapt to life's changes while maintaining the integrity of the original lease agreement.

Common Types of Addendums

Several scenarios commonly give rise to the need for an addendum. Notably, Pet Policies If the original lease prohibits pets or fails to mention them, an addendum can grant permission for a pet, usually alongside conditions related to size, breed, and number of pets, as well as any additional pet deposit required.

Roommate Changes

When a roommate moves out, or a new one moves in, an addendum can officially recognize this change. It might include vetting the new roommate, adjusting the rent split, or other relevant details.

Payment Adjustments

Financial situations can change, necessitating adjustments to payment terms. An addendum could temporarily reduce rent or change payment dates, providing relief during challenging times.

Property Alterations

If you wish to make significant changes to the property, such as painting walls or installing fixtures, an addendum can outline what is allowed and whether these changes need to be reversed at the end of the lease.

Negotiating Addendums

Discussing potential addendums with your landlord starts with clear communication. Here are strategies to facilitate agreement, prepare your case before approaching your landlord, outline why the addendum is necessary and how it could benefit both parties. For instance, allowing a pet might make you more likely to renew your lease, offering the landlord more excellent stability.

Propose Reasonable Terms

Your suggestions should be fair and reasonable, reflecting an understanding of the landlord's concerns. For a pet addendum, propose a reasonable pet deposit or commit to additional cleaning, be open to compromise. Your landlord might have valid concerns or alternative solutions. Finding a middle ground is often crucial to successful negotiations.

Legal Validation of Addendums

For an addendum to be legally binding, it must be crafted and executed with the same formality as the original lease. This means, written format, the addendum should be in writing like the lease. Oral agreements about lease modifications can be challenging to enforce.

Signatures

Both tenant and landlord (or their representatives) must sign the addendum. This mutual agreement signifies consent to the changes.

Consistency with Existing Laws

The addendum must not contain terms that are illegal or that contradict existing laws. For instance, a no-pet policy cannot be enforced if the pet is a legally recognized emotional support animal.

Clarity and Specificity

The addendum should clearly describe the changes to the lease, leaving no room for ambiguity. For example, a pet addendum should specify the type, number, and size of pets allowed, any restrictions, and the pet deposit amount. Incorporating addendums into your lease allows for a dynamic agreement that can adapt to life's inevitable changes. By understanding their purpose, the typical scenarios that necessitate them, and how to negotiate and validate these modifications, you ensure that your lease remains relevant and fair, reflecting the current state of your tenancy. This adaptability fosters a positive landlord–tenant relationship and ensures your rental arrangement continues to meet your evolving needs.

1.9 Subleasing: How to Do It Right

Subleasing can be a valuable option for tenants needing to relocate temporarily without breaking their lease. This section sheds light on subleasing and its distinctions from primary leasing and navigates through its complexities to ensure a successful arrangement.

Understanding Subleasing

Subleasing occurs when an original tenant, or the sublessor, rents out their leased premises to another individual, known as the subtenant. This arrangement does not cancel the original lease but adds a layer to the tenant–landlord relationship. The sublessor steps into a quasi-landlord role for the subtenant while remaining responsible to the original landlord. This setup is handy for tenants who need to move for a few months but intend to return and keep their lease.

Legal and Contractual Considerations

Before pursuing a sublease, it's vital to examine both the legal landscape and the specifics of your lease agreement. Many jurisdictions have laws governing subleasing, and leases often contain clauses that explicitly allow, restrict, or prohibit subleasing.

Key steps include:

Reviewing Your Lease, look for any clauses related to subleasing. You may need to discuss options with your landlord directly if it's prohibited.

Understanding Local Laws

Some areas have tenant-friendly laws that allow subleasing regardless of lease restrictions, but specific conditions may apply.

Landlord Approval

Even if subleasing is permitted under your lease or local law, obtaining explicit consent from your landlord remains a best practice. This step can prevent potential disputes or confusion.

Finding the Right Subtenant

Selecting a trustworthy subtenant is crucial since you remain liable for the rent and condition of the property. Consider employing the following strategies to find a suitable match. Start by asking friends, family, or colleagues if they know someone in need of temporary housing. Personal recommendations can add a layer of trust.

Use Online Platforms

Websites and apps for subletting can expand your search. Be sure to vet candidates carefully, check references, and conduct interviews.

Credit and Background Checks

These checks are standard for traditional leasing and should be applied to subleasing. They can reveal necessary information about a potential subtenant's reliability and financial stability.

Managing a Sublease Agreement

Creating a detailed sublease agreement is non-negotiable. This document should mirror the original lease regarding rules and expectations but be tailored to the subleasing context. Key elements to include are:

Duration of the Sublease

Specify start and end dates, ensuring they align with your original lease term.

Rent and Utilities

Define the amount of rent, who pays it, and how utilities are handled. Decide whether the subtenant pays you directly or if payments go to the landlord.

Damage Deposits

Similar to the original lease, requiring a deposit from your subtenant can help cover potential damages or unpaid rent.

House Rules

Outline any specific conditions or rules of the property, including guest policies, noise levels, and maintenance responsibilities.

Termination Conditions

Establish clear conditions under which the sublease could be terminated early, mirroring the terms of your original lease where possible. For legal protection and clarity, it's wise to have this agreement reviewed by a legal professional familiar with local tenant laws. Keep your landlord in the loop, providing them with a copy of the sublease agreement. This transparency ensures that all parties know the arrangement and can help prevent potential legal issues. In managing a sublease, regular communication with your subtenant and landlord can help ensure the arrangement runs smoothly. Consider setting up monthly check-ins with your sub-tenant to address any concerns or maintenance issues. Likewise, updating your landlord on the status of the sublease can maintain trust and prevent misunderstandings. Subleasing requires careful consideration of legal, financial, and personal factors. By taking the time to understand the nuances of subleasing, carefully selecting a subtenant, and crafting a comprehensive sublease agreement, you can ensure that this arrangement benefits all involved. Whether you're looking to travel, relocate temporarily for work, or any other reason that might take you away from your leased property, subleasing offers a flexible solution that can meet your needs while keeping your original lease intact.

1.10 Digital Leases and E-Signatures: The   Future of Renting

In today's fast-paced world, the shift towards digital solutions has touched nearly every aspect of our lives, including how we rent homes. This evolution towards digital leases and electronic signatures (e-signatures) is transforming the rental process, making it more streamlined and accessible than ever before.

The Rise of Digital Leasing

Gone are the days when signing a lease meant a trip to the land-lord's office with a pen in hand, ready to sign a stack of paperwork. Now, digital platforms have made it possible to review, negotiate, and sign leases anywhere worldwide, provided you have internet access. This shift not only caters to the modern renter's lifestyle, which values convenience and efficiency, but also aligns with the growing demand for contactless transactions, a trend that global health concerns have accelerated.

Understanding E-Signatures

E-signatures are electronic expressions of agreement to the terms within a document. They come in various forms, from typed names at the end of an email to more sophisticated encrypted signatures that use secure e-signature platforms. Legally, e-signatures are recognized as equivalent to traditional handwritten signatures in many jurisdictions, thanks to laws and regulations that have established their validity. This legal recognition underscores the e-signature's role as a secure and enforceable means of executing lease agreements. The process of creating an e-signature usually involves, selecting a document to sign electronically. Authenticating the signer's identity can be as simple as logging into a secure platform or as detailed as answering security questions. Choosing an e-signature format, which might be a drawn representation of one's signature or a digitally generated version. Applying the e-signature to the document indicates agreement with its contents.

Benefits of Digital Leases

The adoption of digital leases and e-signatures brings several advantages that streamline the rental process. The ability to sign a lease anywhere at any time is perhaps the most apparent benefit. This convenience is especially valuable for renters relocating from a different city or country, as it eliminates the need for physical presence during the signing process. Digital leases can be prepared, reviewed, and signed more quickly than traditional paper leases. This efficiency reduces the time it takes to secure a rental, benefiting both renters and landlords. Advanced encryption and authentication methods secure digital leases and e-signatures. Unlike paper documents that can be lost, stolen, or damaged, digital records are stored securely in the cloud, with access controls ensuring only authorized parties can view them.

Environmental Impact

By reducing the need for paper, digital leases contribute to environmental sustainability efforts, aligning with the values of eco-conscious renters and landlords.

Potential Drawbacks and Pitfalls

While digital leases and e-signatures represent a significant advancement in the rental process, they are not without their challenges:

Digital Divide

Not everyone has equal access to technology or the internet, potentially excluding some renters and landlords from fully embracing digital leases.

Privacy Concerns

Storing personal information in digital formats raises questions about data privacy and potential breaches. Renters and landlords must be diligent in selecting platforms that prioritize data security.

Misunderstandings

The ease of clicking a button to sign a digital lease might lead some to skim over important details or terms, increasing the risk of misunderstandings or agreements to unfavorable terms.

Technical Issues

Glitches, software incompatibility, or user error can lead to delays or errors in the signing process. Both parties must have a basic understanding of the technology used to mitigate these risks. Navigating the world of digital leases and e-signatures requires an awareness of their vast potential and limitations. For renters, the convenience and efficiency offered by these digital solutions can significantly simplify the leasing process, making it easier to secure their next home. On the flip side, it's essential to approach these digital agreements with the same level of care and attention as traditional leases, ensuring a clear understanding of the terms and confidence in the security of the chosen platform. As we continue to move towards an increasingly digital world, the evolution of the rental process reflects a broader shift in how we conduct transactions, emphasizing the importance of adaptability, security, and informed decision-making.

Chapter 2

Crafting Your Rental Budget Blueprint

Imagine sitting at your kitchen table, surrounded by piles of bills, a calculator in hand, and a steaming cup of coffee nearby. This scene plays out in countless homes, highlighting a universal challenge: budgeting. When it comes to renting, your budget is more than a list of numbers it reflects your priorities, a roadmap to your financial well-being, and the foundation upon which your stress-free living rests. In this chapter, we'll peel back the layers of creating a rental budget that goes beyond the basics, ensuring it aligns with your lifestyle and prepares you for the road ahead.

The 30% Rule and Its Alternatives

For years, the 30% rule has been a guideline for how much of your income should go towards rent: no more than 30% of your pre-tax earnings. While it's a helpful starting point, it only fits some people's financial picture. High-income earners might afford to spend more, while those with significant debt or lower incomes might find this rule too lenient. Instead, consider a sliding scale approach, adjusting the percentage based on your financial situation. If you're debt-free and have a comfortable savings cushion, perhaps allocating more towards rent for the perfect location makes sense. Conversely, scaling back on rent can accelerate your progress if you're working towards significant financial goals like paying off student loans.

Incorporating Savings and Debt Payments

Your rental budget should account for more than just rent. Savings for emergencies, retirement, personal goals, and debt payments are non-negotiable line items. Think of these as fixed expenses, similar to your rent.

Emergency Fund

Aim to set aside a portion of your monthly income into an emergency fund, ideally reaching a cushion of three to six months' worth of living expenses.

Debt Payments

Factor in minimum debt payments, and if possible, allocate additional funds to tackle high-interest debts more aggressively.

Savings Goals

Whether it's a vacation, a new car, or a down payment on a home, include savings towards your goals as a regular budget item.

Adjusting for Lifestyle and Career Stability

Your lifestyle choices and career stability play pivotal roles in shaping your budget. A freelancer's income might fluctuate, necessitating a lower rent-to-income ratio and a larger emergency fund. Meanwhile, someone with a stable, well-paying job might allocate more towards rent to live in a prime location, cutting down on commute time and increasing leisure time. Reflect on your current lifestyle and career trajectory. How secure is your income? Do you prefer dining out and traveling, or are you a homebody who enjoys cooking? Tailoring your budget to match your lifestyle ensures you're paying attention to the aspects of life you enjoy most or overstressing about rent.

Budgeting for Application Fees and Moving Costs

First-time renters might be surprised by the initial costs of securing a rental. Application fees, security deposits, and first and last month's rent upfront add up quickly. And let's not forget the moving costs: hiring movers, renting a truck, buying packing supplies, and the inevitable expenses of setting up your new place (think internet installation, utility deposits). To navigate these waters smoothly, start saving early. Open a dedicated savings account for moving and application expenses, contributing a small amount each month. When you're ready to move, you'll have a financial cushion to cover these costs without dipping into your emergency fund or racking up credit card debt. Crafting a rental budget that goes beyond just covering your monthly rent is about foresight, planning, and a bit of creativity. It's about ensuring you're prepared for not only the expected costs but also the unexpected while maintaining a lifestyle that brings you joy and fulfillment. In this chapter, we've laid the foundation for a budget that does more than keep you afloat—it helps you thrive in your rental experience. By embracing the principles outlined here, you're not just managing your money; you're taking control of your financial future, setting the stage for a renting experience that's both enjoyable and sustainable. With this blueprint in hand, you're ready to tackle the next steps in your renting journey, equipped with the knowledge and tools to navigate the financial aspects of renting confidently.

2.2 Hidden Costs in Renting and How to Account for Them

Some steps are more subtle in the dance of renting, hidden in the shadows of the prominent monthly rent and utility bills. These less visible expenses, if overlooked, can disrupt your financial rhythm. Understanding these hidden costs ensures you stay in step and make informed decisions that align with your budget.

Maintenance and Repair Contributions

While your landlord typically handles significant repairs, there are scenarios where you might need to contribute financially to the maintenance of the property.

Like Minor Repairs

Small issues like replacing light bulbs or fixing a running toilet might fall under your responsibility.

Wear and Tear

Over time, some wear and tear on the property are inevitable. However, excessive damage beyond everyday use could see you footing the bill for repairs upon moving out.

Enhancements

If you decide to upgrade or add personal touches to the rental, like painting walls or installing new fixtures, these costs come out of your pocket, and you might be required to revert the property to its original state when you leave. Setting aside a small monthly amount into a 'home maintenance' fund can help manage these unexpected costs without causing a dent in your budget.

Amenity Fees and Parking Costs

Living in a rental with amenities like a gym, pool, or community hall can add convenience and luxury. However, these perks often come with additional costs.

Monthly Amenity Fees

Some properties charge extra for access to specific amenities. This fee may be bundled with your rent or listed separately.

Parking Fees

If your rental offers parking, there might be a separate charge for assigned parking spaces or covered parking options. Before signing the lease, clarify what's included in your rent and what additional fees are required. This knowledge prevents surprises and helps you weigh the value of these amenities against their cost.

Renters Insurance Premiums

Renters insurance is an often-overlooked aspect of renting that can save you financially in the event of theft, damage, or liability claims. While only sometimes mandatory, it's a wise investment. Premiums vary based on coverage amount, location, and risk factors, but generally coverage basic policies cover personal property, liability, and additional living expenses if your rental becomes uninhabitable.

Cost

Premiums can range significantly, but expect to budget around $15-$30 monthly for a decent coverage plan. Considering renters insurance in your budget protects your belongings and offers peace of mind.

Late Fees and Other Penalties

Life gets busy, and sometimes payments slip through the cracks. However, overlooking rent due dates can lead to late fees, which vary widely. Fees can be a flat rate or a percentage of your rent, accumulating daily in some cases.

Avoidance

Setting up automatic payments or reminders a few days before your rent is due can help avoid these unnecessary costs. Additionally, understanding the penalties for other lease violations, like unauthorized pets or guests, ensures you steer clear of financial penalties. Shedding light on these hidden costs allows you to navigate the renting landscape more confidently and financially. Considering these considerations will enable you to plan more accurately, ensuring your budget fully encompasses the actual cost of renting.

2.3 Saving Strategies for Your Next Rental Deposit

When securing your next rental, the deposit often stands as one of the first financial hurdles. Unlike monthly rent, which spreads your housing costs over time, a deposit demands a lump sum upfront. This can be daunting, but with a strategic approach to saving, accumulating the necessary funds becomes an achievable goal.

High-Yield Savings Accounts for Deposit Goals

One of the smartest moves you can make is to park your deposit savings in a high-yield savings account (HYSA). Unlike traditional savings accounts, HYSAs offer higher interest rates, meaning your money grows faster without any additional risk. The key here is to start early; even small, regular contributions to your HYSA can quickly add up, thanks to the magic of compound interest. Plus, seeing your savings grow can be a huge motivational boost. Look for accounts with no monthly fees and easy access to your funds when it's time to move. Automate your savings by setting up a direct deposit from your paycheck or a recurring transfer from your checking account. This "set it and forget it" approach ensures you're consistently saving without thinking about it.

Creative Saving Techniques

Adjusting your budget and lifestyle to free up more money for savings doesn't have to mean drastic cuts to your spending. Sometimes, it's the small changes that add up. Here are a few creative strategies.

Round-Up Savings Apps

These apps round up everyday transactions to the nearest dollar and save the difference. For example, if you spend $3.50 on a coffee, the app rounds it up to $4.00 and puts the $0.50 into savings.

52-Week Money Challenge

Save $1 in the first week of the year, $2 in the second, and so on. By the end of the year, you'll have saved $1,378. Adjust the starting amount based on your savings goal and timeframe.

Cutting Subscriptions

Temporarily pause or cancel streaming services, gym memberships, or subscription boxes. Often, we pay for services out of habit rather than necessity.

Borrowing Responsibly for Your Deposit

While saving is the ideal route, sometimes borrowing can be a practical short-term solution for securing your deposit. If you choose to borrow.

Family and Friends

A loan from someone you trust can come with more flexible repayment terms and little to no interest. Just be sure to outline clear repayment terms to avoid any misunderstandings.

Personal Loans

A low-interest personal loan can be a viable option for those with good credit. Shop around for the best rates and consider online lenders in addition to traditional banks. Always calculate the monthly repayment amount to ensure it fits comfortably within your budget, and prioritize paying off the loan as quickly as possible to minimize interest costs.

Deposit Assistance Programs

Various government and non-profit organizations offer programs to help renters with their security deposits. These programs can be lifesavers, particularly for first-time renters, those with limited savings, or individuals recovering from financial setbacks.

Local Housing Authorities

Many cities and counties have programs to assist renters with deposits, often as part of broader affordable housing initiatives.

Non-Profit Organizations

Charities and non-profits sometimes offer grants or interest-free loans to help cover rental deposits.

Community Action Agencies

These agencies provide a range of services to low-income individuals, including assistance with housing costs. To find programs in your area: Start with a simple online search for "rental deposit assistance [your city or county]." Check your local housing authority's website for any available programs. Reach out to local non-profits and charities that focus on housing issues. In conclusion, saving for your next rental deposit requires foresight, discipline, and creativity. Whether through high-yield savings accounts, innovative saving strategies, responsible borrowing, or tapping into assistance programs, the goal is to accumulate the funds you need without compromising your financial health. With the right approach, securing your deposit becomes a dream and a plan in action, paving the way for your next home.

2.4 Budgeting Apps and Tools for Renters

In this digital age, renters have many tools at their fingertips designed to simplify managing finances. From budgeting apps that track every penny to customizable spreadsheets that offer a bird ' s-eye view of your finances, these tools are invaluable for anyone looking to take control of their rental and living expenses. Let's explore how these digital aids can make budgeting less of a chore and more of a strategic advantage in your renting experience.

Top Rated Budgeting Apps for Renters

Navigating the multitude of budgeting apps available can be overwhelming, but several stand out for their user-friendly interfaces, comprehensive tracking capabilities, and specific features tailored to renters. These apps help you manage your monthly rent payments and keep track of utility bills, savings goals, and everyday expenses. Here are a few noteworthy mentions.

Mint

This popular app offers a holistic view of your finances by linking to your bank accounts, tracking spending, and categorizing expenses. Renters will appreciate the ability to set reminders for rent payments and create specific budgets for household expenses.

YNAB (You Need A Budget)

YNAB's approach is based on giving every dollar a job, making it ideal for renters who want to ensure their rent and related expenses are always covered. Its detailed reporting features also help track spending trends over time.

PocketGuard

For renters who frequently ask, "Can I afford this?" PocketGuard provides clarity. It analyzes your income, recurring bills (including rent), and goals to show how much you can safely spend each day.

Customizable Spreadsheets for Comprehensive Budgeting

While apps offer convenience and automation, some renters prefer the flexibility and depth of a good old-fashioned spreadsheet. Spreadsheets allow you to tailor your budgeting system entirely to your needs, incorporating aspects like rent increases, split expenses with roommates, or irregular income. Here's how to set one up effectively, Categories, create categories for all your expenses, ensuring rent, utilities, insurance, and savings have their dedicated sections.

Tracking

Use separate columns to track projected costs against actual spending. This helps with staying on a budget and identifying areas to cut back.

Formulas

Use spreadsheet formulas to calculate totals, differences, and percentages automatically. This reduces manual work and helps highlight trends or issues in your budget. Google Sheets offers templates that can be a great starting point, and Excel's powerful analysis tools can provide deeper insights into your financial habits.

Integrating Rent Payments with Budgeting Tools

For many renters, rent is their most significant monthly expense, so tracking it effectively is crucial. Some budgeting apps and digital banking platforms now offer features that specifically address this need.

Automated Tracking

By connecting your bank account, these tools can recognize and categorize rent payments. This ensures your budget always reflects your most significant recurring expense accurately.

Payment Scheduling

Some apps allow you to schedule your rent payments directly within the platform, ensuring you never miss a due date. This feature often provides notifications a few days before the payment, adding an extra layer of security against late fees. Integrating rent payments into your budgeting tool simplifies managing this expense and ensures it's always accounted for in your financial planning.

Alerts and Reminders for Financial Management

Staying on top of rent payments, bill due dates, and savings goals requires diligence. Here's where setting up alerts and reminders becomes invaluable.

Rent Payment Reminders

Configure your budgeting app or calendar to remind you a few days before your rent is due. This is particularly helpful for renters whose income varies throughout the month, ensuring sufficient funds are available when needed.

Bill Due Alerts

Similar to rent reminders, setting alerts for utility bills, subscription renewals, and other recurring expenses helps avoid late fees and keeps your budget on track.

Savings Goals Notifications

Whether you're saving for a security deposit, an emergency fund, or a big purchase, regular reminders can keep you motivated and focused on your goals. Many budgeting apps offer the ability to set and track specific savings goals, providing periodic updates on your progress. By effectively utilizing these digital tools and strategies, renters can transform the often daunting task of budgeting into a streamlined, efficient process. From ensuring rent and associated costs are always covered to staying disciplined with savings goals, these apps and techniques offer a comprehensive approach to financial management. With the right tools, you're not just tracking numbers but paving the way toward economic stability and peace of mind in your renting journey.

2.5 Utilities 101: What Costs to Expect and How to Save

When settling into a new rental, one of the first encounters with the reality of independent living is the arrival of the utility bills. These costs, while variable, form a significant part of monthly expenses, and their management can either ease or strain your budget. In this section, we'll navigate the waters of utility costs, exploring regional differences, the impact of energy-efficient practices, negotiation tactics with providers, and the debate around utility inclusion in rent. Utilities cover a broad spectrum, including electricity, water, gas, internet, and trash collection. Combining these services ensures your home is comfortable, functional, and connected. Understanding the nuances of these expenses can lead to substantial savings over time.

Average Utility Costs by Region

Utility costs vary widely based on geography, climate, and local infrastructure. For instance, renters in the Northeast might see higher heating bills during the cold months, while those in the South could face steep air conditioning costs in the summer. Cities with robust public utilities might offer water and trash collection at lower rates than areas where these services are privatized.

Electricity

This typically forms the most significant chunk of utility bills. In areas with extreme temperatures, expect this to be higher due to heating and cooling needs.

Water

Generally more stable, but usage policies and rates can affect costs.

Gas

Used for heating and cooking in many homes, varying depending on seasonal usage.

Internet

Costs depend on speed and service packages, with urban areas often having more competitive rates due to higher provider density. Research average utility costs in your area to get a handle on what you might pay. Many local government websites provide this information, or you could ask neighbors or your landlord for estimates.

Energy-Efficient Appliances and Habits

Trimming your utility bills isn't just about using less; it's about using smarter. Energy-efficient appliances and habits can significantly reduce consumption without sacrificing comfort.

LED Lighting

Switching to LED bulbs can save a considerable amount on your electricity bill. They use at least 75% less energy and last 25 times longer than incandescent lighting.

Smart Thermostats

These devices adjust your home's temperature based on your habits and preferences, optimizing energy use and reducing costs.

Water-Saving Fixtures

Low-flow showerheads and faucets can cut your water bill while conserving a precious resource.

Power Strips

Many electronics consume power even when turned off. A power strip can completely cut power to these devices, preventing "vampire" energy usage. Also named brands come with very good surge warranty policies. Adopting these practices reduces monthly bills and contributes to a more sustainable lifestyle.

Negotiating with Utility Providers

Believe it or not, you can often negotiate your utility rates, particularly for services like internet and cable. Providers are keen to keep you as a customer, and with the competitive nature of these markets, you have leverage.

Promotional Rates

Ask for current promotions or discounts. If you've been a loyal customer, mention your history with the company as a bargaining chip.

Bundle Services

Providers often offer bundled packages at a discount if you require multiple services, like internet and cable.

Threaten to Switch

Providers are aware of the competition. Letting them know you're considering other options can prompt them to offer you better rates. While utilities like water and electricity might have fixed providers depending on your location, exploring all available options can ensure you get the best deal possible.

Utility Inclusion in Rent

Some rentals include utilities in the monthly rent. This arrangement can simplify budgeting by consolidating expenses into one payment. However, it's not without its drawbacks. Pros – Simplicity, one bill covers rent and utilities, making financial management more manageable. Predictability - Your expenses remain constant, unaffected by seasonal variations in utility usage. Cons – Lack of Control, since you're not paying for individual usage, there's little incentive for you or your neighbors to conserve, potentially leading to wasteful practices.

Cost

Landlords might charge a premium for the convenience of utility-included rent, possibly costing you more in the long run than if you paid for utilities separately. When considering a utility-included rental, weigh the convenience against the potential for higher costs and assess your usage habits. If you diligently conserve energy, paying for utilities separately might be more economical. Navigating utility costs requires research, negotiation, and adopting efficient habits. You can manage these expenses by understanding the average costs in your area, investing in energy-saving practices, effectively negotiating with service providers, and carefully considering the implications of utility-included rent. This approach ensures comfort and connectivity in your home and supports your broader financial goals, contributing to a balanced, budget-friendly living environment.

2.6 Furnishing Your Rental on a Budget

Making a rental feel like home involves more than paying the rent on time and keeping the lights on. It's about infusing your space with comfort and personality, often through your chosen furniture and decor. However, with the excitement of decorating comes the realization of the costs associated with furnishing a new space. Here, we navigate the path to a beautifully furnished rental without straining your wallet.

Prioritizing Essential Furniture

When furnishing your rental, the key is knowing what you need versus what you want. Starting with the essentials ensures you have a functional living space while also allowing you to spread out the costs over time for less critical pieces.

Bed and Mattress

A good night's sleep is non-negotiable. Investing in a comfortable bed and mattress is a priority.

Sofa

As a centerpiece of the living area, a sturdy and comfortable sofa sets the tone for relaxation and socializing.

Dining Table or Eating Surface

Depending on your space, a dining table or a smaller eating area is crucial for meal times.

Storage Solutions

Whether it's a closet organizer, a dresser, or shelves, having a place to store your belongings helps keep your space tidy and functional. Focusing on these critical pieces initially allows you to gradually add other items, like end tables, lamps, or decorative pieces, as your budget allows.

Finding Deals on Secondhand and Refurbished Items

The world of secondhand and refurbished furniture is a treasure trove for budget-conscious renters. These items can offer significant savings without compromising on quality or style.

Thrift Stores and Flea Markets

These spots can be goldmines for unique, affordable furniture. Regular visits can help you snag great deals.

Online Marketplaces

Platforms like Craigslist, Facebook Marketplace, and Nextdoor frequently list high-quality furniture at a fraction of the retail price. Always inspect items in person when possible to confirm their condition.

Refurbished Furniture Stores

Some stores specialize in selling refurbished or floor-model furniture from popular retailers at discounted prices. These pieces are often in like-new condition. When exploring these options, keep an open mind. Sometimes, a simple fix or a fresh coat of paint can transform a secondhand find into a cherished piece.

DIY Projects to Personalize Your Space

Adding personal touches to your rental doesn't have to mean expensive custom pieces. DIY projects offer a way to inject personality into your space on a budget.

Painting Furniture

A coat of paint can breathe new life into a secondhand piece, matching it to your decor.

Reupholstering

Updating the fabric on a worn-out chair or sofa can transform it into a statement piece.

Repurposing Items

Get creative by turning an old ladder into a bookshelf or a crate into a coffee table. These projects save money and give your space a unique flair. Engaging in DIY projects helps you save money and provides a sense of accomplishment and a deeper connection to your space.

Budgeting for Furniture and Decor

Allocating a specific portion of your budget to furnishing and decorating helps keep your financial goals on track. Set a furnishing budget determines how much you can spend on furniture immediately and over the coming months. Consider setting aside a small amount each month into a furnishing fund.

Prioritize Purchases

Focus on buying essential items first, then gradually add decorative pieces that elevate the look and feel of your space.

Track Spending

Keep an eye on your expenses to ensure you stay within your budget. This can help prevent overspending on impulse buys that might seem like a good deal. By thoughtfully planning your purchases and embracing the hunt for deals, you can create a comfortable, stylish home that reflects your personality without overspending. Remember, furnishing your rental is a process, not a race. Taking your time to find the right pieces at the right price saves money and ensures you end up with a space that truly feels like home.

2.7 Renters Insurance: Protecting Your Belongings for Less

In the renting landscape, there is an often-overlooked ally in safeguarding your personal oasis, renters insurance. This section peels back the layers to reveal why renters insurance isn't just a good idea—it's a critical component of an intelligent renting strategy.

Understanding Renters Insurance Coverage

At its core, renters insurance acts as a safety net designed to protect your personal property against loss or damage due to various events, including theft, fire, and even certain types of water damage. Beyond property protection, most policies include liability coverage, safeguarding you in situations where you're legally responsible for injury to others or damage to their property while in your home. Why is this important? Imagine the financial burden of replacing all your belongings after a fire or covering medical bills if a friend is injured in your home. Renters insurance shoulder this load, offering peace of mind for just pennies a day. It's a small price to pay for significant protection.

Comparing Renters Insurance Policies

Shopping for renters insurance can feel like navigating a maze with countless turns and dead ends. However, breaking it down into manageable steps can simplify the process. Start with coverage needs, and assess the value of your belongings to determine how much coverage you need. Don't forget to consider special items like jewelry or electronics that might require additional coverage.

Check Policy Details

Pay attention to what's covered and under what circumstances. Policies can vary widely regarding deductibles, limits, and excluded events.

Read Reviews and Ratings

Look for customer feedback and ratings on claims process, customer service, and overall satisfaction. Companies with high ratings in these areas are often more reliable and responsive.

Get Multiple Quotes

Prices for similar coverage levels can differ significantly between providers. Obtaining quotes from several companies ensures you find the best rate for the coverage you need. By methodically comparing policies, you're more likely to find one that offers the right balance of cost and protection.

Ways to Lower Your Renters Insurance Premiums

Minimizing the cost of renters insurance without sacrificing essential coverage is easier than you might think. Here are a few strategies to keep premiums in check.

Bundle Policies

Many insurance companies offer discounts when you bundle renters insurance with other policies, such as auto insurance.

Shop Around Annually

Don't settle for automatic renewals without checking for better rates. Market conditions change, and so do your coverage needs.

Increase Your Deductible

Opting for a higher deductible can lower your premium, but ensure it's an amount you can comfortably afford in case of a claim.

Take Advantage of Discounts

Companies often offer discounts for things like smoke detectors, burglar alarms, or even for being a non-smoker. Ask your provider about available discounts. Implementing these tips can lead to meaningful savings, making renters insurance even more affordable.

The Process of Filing a Claim

Should the unexpected happen, knowing how to file a claim can expedite the process and help ensure you're compensated promptly and fairly. Here's a basic outline of the steps involved:

Immediate Actions

In case of theft, report the incident to the police immediately. For damage, take steps to prevent further loss, such as covering broken windows or turning off water.

Document Everything

Take photos or videos of the damage and create a detailed inventory of lost or damaged items, including their value. This documentation is critical in supporting your claim.

Contact Your Insurance Company

Notify your insurer as soon as possible to start the claims process. Be prepared to provide details of the incident and any documentation you've gathered.

Review the Settlement Offer

Once the insurance company assesses your claim, they'll offer a settlement. Review this carefully to ensure it covers the cost of replacing or repairing your belongings. Navigating a claim with thorough preparation and clear communication can make a potentially stressful situation more manageable, helping you recover and return to normal life more quickly. Renters insurance is a testament to the adage, "better safe than sorry." With its comprehensive coverage, affordability, and the peace of mind, it's an essential component of an intelligent renting plan. By understanding what renters insurance covers, knowing how to shop for the right policy, employing strategies to lower your premiums, and familiarizing yourself with the claims process, you can protect yourself and your belongings against life's unexpected turns.

2.8 Negotiating Rent: Strategies for Getting the Best Deal

Securing a rental at a great price isn't just about luck; it involves a well-crafted strategy, a bit of research, and understanding the right timing. This section aims to equip you with the tools necessary for negotiating a lower rent, making your rental experience enjoyable and financially savvy.

Leveraging Market Research in Negotiations

Before you negotiate, arm yourself with knowledge about the current rental market. This information is a powerful tool that can provide leverage during discussions. Here's how to go about it. Spend time browsing listings for similar properties in the area. Note the average prices for comparable rentals. Look for trends. Are there many vacancies? This could indicate a renter's market where landlords might be more willing to negotiate to fill their properties quickly. Gather data on how long properties have been listed. Longer times on the market might make landlords more receptive to negotiation. Presenting this research during your negotiation shows the landlord you're informed and serious. It also subtly hints that you have other options, giving you an advantage.

Timing Your Lease for Optimal Rates

<u>When,</u> you choose to sign a new lease it can have a significant impact on the rent you'll pay. Here's why timing matters. Winter months often see fewer people moving, leading to lower demand. Landlords might be more willing to negotiate during this time to avoid vacancies. Conversely, the summer months typically experience a surge in rental activity, driving prices up. If you have flexible moving schedules, aim for a late fall or early winter move. This strategy requires planning and might only sometimes align with your needs, but when it does, it can lead to considerable savings.

Negotiation Do's and Don'ts

Navigating the negotiation process requires a balance of assertiveness and diplomacy. Here are some key points to keep in mind. Communicate clearly and respectfully. Your aim is to build a positive relationship with your landlord from the start. Be honest about your budget constraints. If a proposed rent is beyond what you can afford, say so. Offer something in return. Perhaps you're willing to sign a longer lease or pay a few months' rent upfront.

Don't start with a low-ball offer. This can come off as disrespectful and might sour the negotiation. Approach the conversation with a collaborative mindset. Take it personally if your initial requests are not met. Negotiation is a process, and some back-and-forth is to be expected.

Building a Case for Lower Rent

When asking for a reduction in rent, it's crucial to present a compelling case. This involves more than just stating your desire for a lower price. Instead, highlight your strengths as a tenant. If you have a stable income, a solid rental history, and references, be sure the landlord knows. If you've noticed issues with the property that need addressing, suggest that a lower rent could account for these. However, do this tactfully to avoid implying that the property isn't worth the asking price. Propose how a lower rent could benefit the landlord in the long run. For example, a longer lease provides income stability, potentially making a slight reduction in monthly rent worthwhile. This approach shows that you're not just asking for a discount but offering something of value in return. Negotiating rent requires a blend of preparation, timing, and effective communication. By entering these discussions with a solid understanding of the rental market, a strategic approach to timing, and a clear case for why a lower rent is mutually beneficial, you're well-positioned to secure a deal that fits your budget. Remember, the goal is not just to reduce costs but to establish a positive, long-term relationship with your landlord.

2.9 The Impact of Location on Your Rental Budget

Choosing where to live isn't just about selecting a property that meets your aesthetic and spatial needs; it's about understanding how location influences every aspect of your rental experience, especially your finances. From the trade-offs between rent costs and location benefits to the unforeseen expenses tied to your neighborhood choice, let's peel back the layers on how location impacts your rental budget.

Location vs. Rent Trade-Offs

When you're weighing the merits of various neighborhoods, it's easy to get caught up in the allure of trendy areas or those closest to the city center. However, these locations often command higher rent, reflecting their demand and convenience. Before you commit, consider what you're gaining against what you're giving up financially. Living in a bustling downtown area might mean more accessible access to work, entertainment, and dining, but could these conveniences justify the premium in rent? Conversely, opting for a more affordable rental in a suburb or a less central area might lower your monthly expenses, but consider the lifestyle changes this might entail. Are you comfortable with longer commutes or having fewer amenities within walking distance? Balancing these factors requires clearly understanding your priorities and how much you're willing to adjust your budget to accommodate them.

Transportation Costs and Commuting Considerations

Your rental location directly influences your transportation costs, making it a critical factor in your budgeting process. Here's how. Living centrally might allow you to walk or bike to work, significantly reducing or eliminating transportation costs from your budget. Choosing a rental further from your workplace or city hotspots could mean higher expenses related to car payments, gas, public transit passes, or ride-sharing services. Consider the time cost as well. Longer commutes add to your expenses and eat into your personal time. Is the trade-off worth the lower rent? Mapping out your regular commutes and calculating the associated costs can clarify how location affects your transportation budget and overall living expenses.

Local Amenities and Their Value

The charm of a neighborhood often lies in its amenities — parks, gyms, cafes, and grocery stores all add to the appeal of a location. However, accessibility to these amenities can also affect your rental budget in less obvious ways. Proximity to high-quality amenities might lead to higher rent prices, reflecting the desirability of living within easy reach of these facilities. On the flip side, consider the savings and convenience of having essentials and leisure options just a short walk away. Could this reduce your reliance on transportation, lowering overall living costs? Additionally, living near comprehensive amenities can enhance your quality of life, which, while harder to quantify, is a significant factor in the value you derive from a location. Evaluating the availability and importance of local amenities to your lifestyle helps you make an informed choice that balances cost with convenience and satisfaction.

Safety and Neighborhood Reputation

Finally, the safety and reputation of a neighborhood play non-negotiable roles in determining where you choose to live. While it's tempting to prioritize budget-friendly options, compromising on safety can have far-reaching implications. Safer neighborhoods might command higher rents, but the peace of mind and security they offer are invaluable. This is especially true if you frequently come home late or have or plan to have children. The reputation of an area affects not just your day-to-day life but also your future potential. Investing in a rental in an up-and-coming area with a solid safety record can be beneficial in the long run as property values and quality of life improve. Researching crime rates, talking to potential neighbors, and visiting the area at different times can give you a better sense of what to expect and whether the location aligns with your safety standards and budget. Incorporating safety considerations into your location decision ensures that your chosen home offers financial suitability and a secure and comfortable environment for you to thrive. Selecting the right location for your rental goes beyond mere preference. It involves balancing financial considerations, lifestyle needs, and personal safety. Understanding how these facets interact with your rental budget allows you to make choices that align with your financial goals while ensuring a fulfilling living experience. Poised at the intersection of cost, convenience, and comfort, the decision of where to rent is pivotal, shaping not just your monthly expenses but the fabric of your daily life.

2.10 Splitting Costs and Responsibilities: Navigating Financials and Responsibilities with Roommates

Living with roommates is a strategic way to reduce individual living costs, enabling people to allocate more of their budget towards savings, debt repayment, or leisure. However, this arrangement necessitates a transparent system for dividing expenses to maintain harmony and financial fairness. Here, we explore methods for sharing costs, effective communication, utilizing digital tools for financial management, and resolving disputes should they arise.

Setting Up a Fair Expense Sharing System

Creating a fair system for splitting rent and utilities begins with transparency and agreement on what 'fair' means to everyone involved. Consider these steps:

Equal vs. Proportional Split

Decide whether costs will be divided equally or proportionally based on room size, private bathrooms, or personal income levels.

Fixed vs. Variable Expenses

Differentiate between fixed expenses like rent and variable ones like utilities and groceries. Agree on how each category will be handled and split.

Regular Review

Schedule periodic reviews of your expense-sharing arrangement to ensure it continues to meet everyone's needs and adjust for any significant changes in living situations or financial standings.

Communication Strategies for Financial Matters

Open and honest communication is the backbone of successfully managing shared finances. Here's how to keep the dialogue constructive:

Initial Agreement

Early in the roommate relationship, have a detailed discussion about everyone's financial situations, expectations, and any concerns.

Regular Check-ins

Hold monthly meetings to review expenses, discuss any issues, and plan for upcoming costs. This keeps everyone informed and avoids surprises.

Conflict Resolution

Approach financial disagreements with a problem-solving mind-set, focusing on finding a solution that works for all parties rather than assigning blame.

Tools and Apps for Managing Shared Expenses

Thankfully, technology offers solutions that simplify tracking and splitting shared expenses. Apps like Splitwise, Venmo, and Zelle can streamline the process:

Expense Tracking

Use apps designed for roommates to log shared expenses, track who owes what, and send payment reminders.

Easy Transfers

Choose payment apps that allow for immediate funds transfers between roommates, making it simple to settle up at any moment.

Shared Accounts

For households committed to long-term cohabitation, consider a joint bank account for shared expenses, ensuring all contributions and payments are transparent.

Dealing with Financial Disputes Among Roommates

Even with the best plans, disputes can arise. Addressing these conflicts promptly and fairly is crucial:

Documentation

Keep detailed records of all agreements and expenses. This can help clarify misunderstandings and provide a clear basis for discussions.

Mediation

If a resolution isn't easily reached, consider involving a neutral third party to mediate the dispute, offering an unbiased perspective.

Plan for Change

If disagreements persist, be prepared to revisit your living arrangement and financial agreements. Sometimes, adjustments are necessary to maintain peace and economic health. Navigating the financial dynamics of living with roommates involves more than just splitting bills. It's about establishing a system that respects everyone's financial boundaries while fostering a collaborative living environment. Through clear agreements, open communication, and the help of digital tools, roommates can create a balanced and equitable approach to shared living expenses. This ensures a harmonious home and supports each individual's financial goals, contributing to a more secure and enjoyable shared living experience.

As we wrap up this exploration into the complexities of managing finances within shared living situations, it's evident that success lies in the blend of structure, communication, and flexibility. By adopting a system that fairly allocates expenses, maintaining open lines of dialogue about financial matters, leveraging technology to streamline processes, and addressing disputes with a focus on solutions, roommates can easily navigate their shared financial responsibilities. This approach lays a solid foundation for a financially balanced household and one that's harmonious and conducive to personal growth. As we transition from the specific considerations of shared living arrangements to broader financial strategies for renters, it becomes clear that transparency, communication, and mutual respect are universally applicable. These core values facilitate smoother financial interactions with roommates and serve as guiding principles in all financial dealings within the rental landscape.

Chapter 3

Tenant Rights -Your Shield and Armor

Picture this you've just moved into your dream apartment. It's got the perfect view, the ideal location, and just the right amount of space. But soon, you notice the heater doesn't work, and the landlord isn't responding to your calls. What do you do? This scenario, while frustrating, isn't uncommon. That's where knowing your rights as a tenant comes into play. It's not just about paying rent on time; it's about understanding the protections and entitlements at your disposal.

Understanding Basic Tenant Rights

Rights to privacy, safety, and habitability are the pillars supporting every tenant's experience. Here's what they entail:

Privacy

Your landlord can't barge in whenever they please. They must provide notice, usually 24 to 48 hours, before entering your rental, except in emergencies.

Safety

Landlords must ensure the property meets safety standards. Think smoke detectors, secure locks, and clear emergency exits.

Habitability

A rental should be fit to live in. This means working plumbing, heating, and electricity and being free from pests. Knowing these rights is like having a shield; it offers protection. But to use it effectively, you need to understand its scope and limitations.

State-Specific Rights

Tenant rights aren't one-size-fits-all. They can vary widely depending on where you live. For instance, some states have stringent regulations about security deposit returns, while others are more lenient. Here's how to stay informed. Check your state's government website for a tenant's handbook or guide. Visit local housing authority offices or their websites. Talk to a local tenants' rights group. Understanding the rights specific to your state is like customizing your armor. It ensures your protection is tailored to the local landscape.

The Right to a Habitable Home

A habitable home is more than just a roof over your head; it's where all critical systems work as they should. Here's what generally qualifies a rental as habitable. No water leaks or severe mold problems. Heating systems work during cold months. Electrical systems are safe and functional. If your rental falls short, you have the right to request repairs. Document the issues with photos and communicate with your landlord in writing. If the problems still need to be addressed, your state's laws may allow you to withhold rent or make the repairs yourself and deduct the cost from your rent. However, the specifics can vary, so it's crucial to know the procedures and protections in your area.

Resolving Disputes with Landlords

Sometimes, despite your best efforts, issues arise. Here's a strategy for dealing with disputes.

Start with Communication

Often, a solution is just a conversation away. Approach your landlord calmly and clearly with your concerns.

Document Everything

Keep records of all communications, repairs requested and completed, and any other relevant interactions.

Know When to Seek Help

If disputes can't be resolved directly, it might be time to get external help. Local tenant unions, legal aid societies, or a mediator can offer assistance. Imagine these steps as your strategy on the battlefield. Each move is calculated to protect your rights while aiming for a peaceful resolution.

Visual Element

Here is a check list from the things we covered earlier.

1. **Research the neighborhood and location of the property:** Check crime rates, proximity to amenities, schools, and public transportation.

2. **Check the condition of the property:** Inspect for any damages, pests, and safety hazards. Consider hiring a professional inspector for a thorough evaluation.

3. **Review the lease agreement:** Make sure you understand all terms and conditions, including rent amount, duration of lease, security deposit, maintenance responsibilities, and pet policies.

4. **Verify the landlord or property management company:** Check online reviews, references, and any complaints filed with the Better Business Bureau.

5. **Review the rental history of the property:** Ask for references from previous tenants to get an idea of the landlord's responsiveness to maintenance issues and overall satisfaction.

6. **Verify the legality of the rental:** Ensure that the property is in compliance with local housing codes and regulations. You can consult

with local housing authorities or tenant advocacy organizations for guidance.

7. Consider getting renter's insurance: Protect yourself and your belongings in case of theft, damage, or liability issues. Consult with insurance providers for quotes and coverage options.

8. Consult with a real estate attorney: If you have any legal questions or concerns about the lease agreement, seek advice from a professional experienced in real estate law.

By following this checklist and consulting with relevant references, you can make an informed decision before leasing a property.

Understanding your rights as a tenant doesn't just prevent headaches; it empowers you to stand up for yourself and make informed decisions. Whether it's ensuring your rental is safe and habitable or knowing how to handle disputes with your landlord, these rights are your shield and armor in renting.

3.2 Landlord Obligations:

What They Can and Can't Do

Navigating the waters of a landlord-tenant relationship involves recognizing not just what you're entitled to as a tenant but also understanding the responsibilities resting on the shoulders of your landlord. This mutual awareness fosters a respectful and legally compliant living arrangement. In this section, we dissect the key areas of landlord obligations, shedding light on what they must do to make your rental experience safe and enjoyable.

Maintenance and Repairs

A landlord's duty to maintain the property in a safe and habitable condition is not just a courtesy, it's a legal requirement, which encompasses:

Prompt responses to repair requests that affect the property's habitability.

Regular upkeep of common areas and systems such as HVAC, plumbing, and electrical to prevent hazards.

Adherence to building codes and health regulations to ensure the safety and well-being of tenants.

It's worth noting that while landlords must address significant issues, the nuances of what constitutes "significant" can vary, highlighting the importance of clear communication and setting realistic expectations from both ends.

Respecting Tenant Privacy

The balance between a landlord's right to access their property for inspections, repairs, or showings and a tenant's right to privacy is delicate. Here's what the law typically stipulates:

Notice Requirement: Landlords must provide advance notice—commonly 24 to 48 hours—before entering a tenant's unit.

Emergency Situations: Immediate entry is permitted without notice only in emergencies, such as a fire or severe water leak. Reasonable Frequency: Visits should be kept reasonably, avoiding harassment or unnecessary disturbance to the tenant's peaceful enjoyment of the property. This respect for privacy aligns with legal standards and contributes to a trusting landlord-tenant relationship.

Handling Security Deposits

The management of security deposits is a common area of misunderstanding and conflict. Landlords are obliged to:

Collect security deposits up to a legally specified limit, often not exceeding one or two months' rent.

Store deposits

In some states in a separate, interest-bearing account, ensuring the funds are protected and accountable. Provide an itemized list of any deductions from the deposit for repairs or cleaning beyond normal wear and tear upon the tenant's departure. Return the remaining deposit within a state-specified timeframe, ranging from 14 to 60 days after the lease ends. By adhering to these protocols, landlords comply with the law and demonstrate integrity and fairness in their financial dealings with tenants.

Discrimination and Fair Housing

The principle of non-discrimination is at the heart of a just and equitable housing system. Landlords must navigate this aspect with a clear understanding and commitment to fairness. This means:

Adhering to the Fair Housing Act prohibits discrimination based on race, color, national origin, religion, sex, familial status, or disability.

Applying consistent criteria to all applicants when screening for tenancy to avoid bias or prejudice.

Making reasonable accommodations for tenants with disabilities, such as allowing service animals even in a "no pets" property or providing designated parking.

Compliance with these laws is a legal must and cultivates an inclusive and welcoming community for all tenants. By meeting these obligations, landlords ensure compliance with the law and lay the foundation for a positive and respectful relationship with their tenants. This dynamic contributes significantly to both parties' overall satisfaction and security, making the rental experience mutually beneficial.

3.3 Dealing with Repairs

Who's Responsible?

Navigating the waters of maintenance and repairs in a rental can sometimes feel like decoding an ancient script. It's all about understanding who holds the quill – the tenant or the landlord? Here, we will unravel this script, laying bare the roles each party plays in keeping the rented abode in shipshape.

Tenant vs. Landlord Repair Obligations

At the heart of rental maintenance lies a division of responsibility that, while generally standard, can have nuances based on your lease agreement.

Landlord's Domain

Structural integrity, including the roof, walls, and windows, and essential services like plumbing, heating, and electrical systems, fall squarely on the landlord's shoulders. Essentially, the landlord typically takes the lead if it's a matter of safety or habitability.

Tenant's Terrain

On the flip side, the tenant usually handles minor upkeep. This could include changing light bulbs, replacing smoke detector batteries, or managing the property's cleanliness. Think of these as the small cogs that keep the daily life running smoothly. Misunderstandings can arise, but referring to your lease and local housing laws can usually clarify who's responsible for what.

Requesting Repairs

Knowing how to formally request a fix is crucial when a repair is beyond the tenant's scope and falls into the landlord's responsibilities.

Written Notice

Always submit repair requests in writing. This document should detail the issue, how it affects you, and a reasonable deadline for the repair. Email serves well, providing a timestamp for your records.

Follow-Up

Follow up with a polite reminder if the initial request goes unanswered. Sometimes, communications need to be noticed.

Documentation

Keep a log of all communications regarding the repair. This can be invaluable if the issue escalates or you need to prove that requests were made and ignored.

This process isn't just about paperwork; it's about creating a clear trail that shows you've taken the proper steps.

Withholding Rent for Unaddressed Repairs

A more drastic step, withholding rent, is sometimes considered when urgent repairs go unaddressed. However, tread carefully:

Legal Grounds

Most jurisdictions allow rent withholding only under specific conditions, such as when a repair issue significantly impacts habitability.

Partial Withholding

In some cases, you might be entitled to withhold a portion of the rent equivalent to the diminished value of your rental due to the issue.

Escrow Account

Rather than simply not paying, the recommended course is to deposit the withheld rent into an escrow account, demonstrating your willingness to pay once the issue is resolved. Before taking this step, please consult with a legal professional or a tenants' rights organization to ensure it's done correctly and legally.

Emergency Repairs

Situations may arise where an urgent repair is needed, and the landlord needs to be more responsive. In such cases, If the situation poses an immediate risk to your safety or the integrity of the property (like a burst pipe), you may need to act swiftly.

Reasonable Costs

Should you need to commission the repair, ensure the costs are reasonable. Keep all receipts and documentation of the issue and repair process.

Reimbursement

Notify your landlord about the emergency and the action taken, and request reimbursement as soon as possible. If the repair was indeed the landlord's responsibility, you are typically entitled to be repaid.

These steps are not about bypassing your landlord but ensuring safety and habitability when immediate action is necessary.

In the dance of rental maintenance, knowing the steps - whether a landlord's leap or a tenant's turn - ensures the music plays on harmoniously. Keeping open lines of communication, understanding the choreography of responsibilities, and knowing when and how to take action keeps both parties moving to the same rhythm.

3.4 Security Deposits

How to Ensure You Get Yours Back

When you first step into a new rental, the excitement can sometimes overshadow the practicalities, such as the security deposit. This initial financial commitment isn't just a formality but a significant part of your renting agreement that can impact your wallet. Understanding how to navigate the intricacies of security deposits will equip you with the knowledge to protect this investment.

Pre-Move-In Documentation

The moment you cross the threshold of your new home before you even unpack a single box, take the time for a thorough walkthrough. Documenting the rental's condition is crucial. This isn't about nitpicking; it's about safeguarding your deposit against claims for damages you didn't cause.

Photographs and Videos

A picture is worth a thousand words and, in this case, potentially hundreds of dollars. Take clear, date-stamped photos or videos of every room, focusing on existing damages, no matter how minor they seem.

Checklist

Many landlords provide a move-in checklist. If so, use it to note any discrepancies. If not, create your own, detailing the condition of items like carpets, walls, appliances, and windows.

Landlord Confirmation

Share your findings with your landlord. Requesting their written acknowledgment creates a mutual understanding of the property's condition at move-in.

Legal Reasons for Deposit Deductions

Landlords hold security deposits as a safety net against various potential losses, but they can't just deduct at whim. Knowing what constitutes a valid deduction helps you assess any claims against your deposit.

Unpaid Rent

This is a straightforward reason for deductions. If you leave with rent outstanding, expect it to come out of your deposit.

Damages Beyond Normal Wear and Tear

Normal wear is anticipated, but significant damage, such as wall holes or broken fixtures, is deductible.

Cleaning Costs

If you leave your rental in a state requiring beyond standard cleaning, those costs can also be deducted. Understanding these conditions puts you in a better position to assess any deductions fairly and ensures that you maintain the property in a manner that minimizes potential charges.

Disputing Unfair Deductions

Sometimes, disagreements arise over what constitutes fair wear and tear or the necessity and cost of repairs. If you find yourself facing what you believe to be unfair deductions from your security deposit, taking a structured approach can help you contest these claims.

Review Your Lease

Your lease should outline conditions related to the security deposit. Use this as your first reference point.

Written Challenge

If deductions seem unjust, draft a concise letter to your landlord outlining your dispute. Include references to your move-in documentation to support your claims.

Mediation Services

If direct resolution proves challenging, consider mediation. Many communities offer free or low-cost services to help resolve such disputes without escalating to legal action.

State Laws Governing Security Deposits

Security deposit rules are unique; they vary from state to state, covering aspects like maximum amounts, holding requirements, and return timelines.

Caps on Deposits

Some states limit the amount a landlord can charge for a security deposit, often tied to the rental amount.

Interest Payments

In certain jurisdictions, landlords must place security deposits in interest-bearing accounts and may need to return the deposit plus interest.

Return Timelines

States dictate specific timelines by which landlords must return security deposits post-tenancy, ranging from 14 to 60 days, along with itemized lists of any deductions. Familiarizing yourself with your state's specific regulations ensures you know your rights and obligations concerning your security deposit. This knowledge prepares you for discussions and potential disputes with your landlord and empowers you to take proactive steps to protect your financial interests. Navigating the realm of security deposits with a clear strategy enhances your chances of receiving your full deposit back at the end of your tenancy. From the moment you move in, taking detailed documentation sets a baseline for the property's condition, against which any future claims can be measured. Understanding the legal framework within which deductions can be made helps you evaluate the validity of your landlord's claims, and knowing how to dispute unfair deductions equips you with the tools to advocate for yourself. Finally, arming yourself with knowledge about the specific laws and regulations governing security deposits in your state provides a solid foundation for ensuring that your rights are respected and that you can confidently address any issues that arise regarding your security deposit.

3.5 Privacy Rights

Understanding Your Entitlements

In the realm of renting, your living space is your sanctuary—a place where the outside world's hustle fades into the background, offering peace. Yet, this peaceful enjoyment hinges on mutual respect for privacy, a concept enshrined in tenant law yet often navigated through the murky waters of everyday interactions with landlords and property management.

The Right to Quiet Enjoyment

Though seemingly straightforward, this right encompasses a broad spectrum of protections against disturbances. It assures that unnecessary noise, disruptions, or intrusions don't wreck your enjoyment of the property. Whether it's the landlord's responsibility to handle noisy neighbors or to keep their visits to a minimum, this right forms the bedrock of your peaceful living environment. Here's how you can ensure it's honored.

Noise Complaints

If external noises disrupt your peace, document the disturbances and communicate with your landlord. They may not directly control external sources but can take steps to mitigate issues, especially if the noise comes from within the property.

Landlord Communication

Should your landlord's actions directly infringe on this right, a diplomatically worded letter can remind them of your entitlement to quiet enjoyment, encouraging them to schedule visits or maintenance work at more appropriate times.

Landlord Entry Regulations

While landlords have legitimate reasons to enter a rental unit, such as performing repairs or conducting inspections, this access isn't unfettered. Here are the circumstances under which a landlord can lawfully cross the threshold of your private living space.

Routine Inspections and Repairs

Landlords can enter for maintenance and inspections with adequate notice. This notice period varies but aims to respect your privacy while allowing property upkeep.

Emergency Situations

Immediate dangers to the property or its inhabitants justify entry without prior notice. Think burst pipes or fire.

Legal Proceedings

Landlords may enter under specific legal orders or processes in rare cases, such as evictions or legal inspections. Asserting your rights while understanding the exceptions helps maintain a respectful balance between tenant privacy and landlord responsibilities.

Surveillance and Privacy

In today's digital age, surveillance technologies present new privacy challenges. While landlords might install cameras in common areas for security, the boundaries of this practice are strictly drawn.

Common Areas

Cameras may be placed in hallways, parking lots, or lobbies for security. However, their positioning should never compromise the privacy of individual dwellings.

Rental Units

Surveillance devices within your rental without consent violate your privacy rights. If you discover unauthorized surveillance, document the evidence and address it immediately with your landlord or legal authorities. Understanding where the line is drawn between security measures and invasive surveillance ensures your privacy is not unjustly breached.

Protecting Your Personal Information

In the digital footprint era, safeguarding your personal information becomes another facet of your privacy rights as a tenant.
From the application process to everyday communications, here's
how to ensure your data remains confidential.

Secure Channels

Opt for secure communication channels for sharing sensitive
information. Encrypted emails or tenant portals are safer than text
messages or unsecured emails.

Personal Data Sharing

Be cautious about what personal information you share. Unless
legally required, sensitive details should remain confidential.

Identity Theft Protection

Monitor your credit reports and financial accounts for signs
of unauthorized activity, especially if you've shared personal information with landlords or property management. Vigilance in
protecting your personal information complements the physical
privacy rights afforded to you as a tenant, creating a comprehensive shield against intrusions into your private life. In navigating
the landscape of tenant privacy rights, a proactive approach paired
with a clear understanding of your entitlements and the boundaries of landlord access ensures your rental remains a haven of
peace and privacy. This knowledge empowers you to advocate for

your rights and fosters a respectful and legally sound relationship with your landlord, ensuring your living space is your own.

3.6 Handling Evictions

Know Your Legal Avenues

Evictions are not just a mere inconvenience; they can significantly disrupt your life, affecting everything from your mental well-being to your financial health. However, not all evictions are lawful, and understanding the eviction process, valid reasons for eviction, and how to contest an unlawful eviction can arm you with the knowledge needed to navigate potentially turbulent waters.

Understanding the Eviction Process

The eviction process typically starts with a notice from the landlord specifying the reason for eviction and the time frame in which you must either rectify the issue or vacate the premises. Should you choose not to comply, the landlord can file an eviction lawsuit. Importantly, until a court order is obtained, the landlord cannot forcibly remove you from the property. Here are the key steps.

Notice to Vacate

Often, this is the first step in the eviction process, where the landlord informs you of the intent to evict.

Court Filing

If the issue isn't resolved, the landlord may proceed to file an eviction case in court.

Hearing

You'll be summoned to court, where both parties can present their case.

Judgment

The court will issue a judgment, which could either favor the landlord, resulting in your eviction, or you, allowing you to stay. Throughout this process, it's critical that you remain engaged, responding to communications and attending all hearings, as failure to do so can result in a default judgment against you.

Valid Grounds for Eviction

Landlords cannot evict tenants whimsically or out of retaliation. There are specific, lawful reasons for eviction, including, Non-payment of Rent. This is the most straightforward reason for eviction. If rent isn't paid, landlords can initiate eviction proceedings.

Lease Violations

This could range from having pets in a no-pet property to unauthorized occupants. Violating any lease terms can be grounds for eviction.

Illegal Activities

Conducting illegal activities within the rental unit is a serious breach that can lead to eviction.

Expiration of Lease

If your lease term has ended and the landlord chooses not to renew it, they can request you to vacate the property. Understanding these grounds can help you assess your situation and determine if an eviction notice you've received aligns with lawful reasons.

Fighting an Unlawful Eviction

If you believe an eviction notice or process is unjust, you have avenues to contest it.

Documentation

Gather all relevant documents, including your lease, any notices you've received, communication with your landlord, and
evidence of payments or repairs.

Legal Representation

Consider hiring a lawyer specializing in tenant law to help
navigate the legal system and present your case effectively.

Tenant Rights Organizations

Many cities have organizations that offer support and resources
to tenants facing eviction. They can provide guidance on your
rights and the best course of action. Fighting an eviction can be
daunting, but with the proper preparation and support, you can
effectively contest an unjust eviction.

Resources and Assistance for Facing Eviction

Facing an eviction is stressful, but you're not alone. Numerous
resources can assist.

Legal Aid

Many non-profit organizations offer free or low-cost legal services to tenants facing eviction. They can provide legal advice, representation, and support throughout the process.

Housing Counselors

Certified housing counselors can offer advice on evictions and may help you understand your options and rights.

Local Government Programs

Some local governments have programs to assist tenants in eviction proceedings, including mediation services and financial assistance for those who qualify. Seeking out these resources can provide much-needed support and guidance, helping you navigate through the eviction process with a clearer understanding of your rights and options. In the landscape of tenant-landlord relationships, evictions represent a significant challenge. However, you can better navigate these situations with knowledge of the eviction process, an understanding of valid grounds for eviction, strategies to contest unlawful evictions, and awareness of available resources. Whether through self-advocacy, legal representation, or seeking support from tenant rights organizations, there are pathways to contest and potentially overturn an unjust eviction. Remember, knowledge is your ally, and understanding your legal rights and avenues can make all the difference when facing eviction challenges.

3.7 Discrimination and Fair Housing

Standing Up for Your Rights

Finding a place that feels like home is a goal shared by many, but the road to securing that perfect spot can sometimes be marred by unfair practices and discrimination. Here, we aim to arm you with the knowledge to recognize when discrimination occurs in the rental process, understand the protective laws in place, and know how to assert your rights confidently.

Recognizing Housing Discrimination

Discrimination in housing isn't always overt; sometimes, it's the subtle cues or the unexplained rejections that signal unfair treatment. Be vigilant for signs such as inconsistent Information. If the details or availability of a rental suddenly change upon your visit or inquiry, this could be a red flag.

Refusal to Rent

Being outright denied the opportunity to rent without a valid, clearly explained reason.

Unequal Treatment

Notice if the landlord seems to set stricter terms or higher standards for you than other tenants or applicants.

Steering

Landlords or agents might try to direct you towards or away from specific neighborhoods or properties based on discriminatory reasons. Awareness is the first step. Recognizing these actions as potential discrimination empowers you to seek further advice and take action if necessary.

Fair Housing Laws

The Fair Housing Act is the cornerstone of your defense against housing discrimination. This federal law prohibits discrimination in renting, selling, or financing homes based on race, color, national origin, religion, sex, familial status, or disability. Many states and cities have expanded these protections to include additional categories such as sexual orientation, gender identity, and source of income. Here's a breakdown:

Federal Protections

The Fair Housing Act provides nationwide protections, ensuring a baseline of rights for all.

State and Local Laws

These can offer broader protections. It's crucial to check the specific laws in your area as they can provide additional layers of security against discrimination. Understanding these laws puts a powerful tool at your disposal, fortifying your position when navigating the rental market.

Filing a Discrimination Complaint

If you suspect you've been a victim of discrimination, taking formal action is a step towards seeking justice for yourself and preventing future injustices against others. Here's how to proceed:

Document Everything

Keep detailed records of all interactions, including dates, times, names, and specifics of the discriminatory behavior.

File a Complaint with HUD

The U.S. Department of Housing and Urban Development (HUD) oversees Fair Housing complaints. You can file a complaint online, by mail, or by phone.

State and Local Agencies

Many areas have their fair housing agencies that can process complaints. Sometimes, filing with these agencies can be faster, and they might offer additional protections.

Legal Action

Consider consulting with an attorney specializing in fair housing issues. They can offer guidance on the merits of your case and the potential for legal recourse. Each step strengthens the foundation of fair housing for all, ensuring that discriminatory practices do not go unchecked.

Support and Resources for Victims of Discrimination

Discrimination can be isolating, but numerous organizations and resources are dedicated to supporting individuals in these situations. Turning to these sources can provide guidance, emotional support, and advocacy:

HUD Counseling

HUD offers housing counseling services, including assistance with discrimination issues.

Fair Housing Advocates

Organizations dedicated to fair housing often provide free legal advice, advocacy, and assistance with filing complaints.

Legal Aid Societies

These organizations offer free or low-cost legal services to those who qualify, including representation in discrimination cases.

Community Groups

Local community organizations can be valuable sources of support and may offer additional resources or referrals. Engaging with these resources helps you navigate the complexities of asserting your rights and connects you with a community committed to fairness and equality in housing. Facing housing discrimination is a challenge no one should have to endure. By recognizing the signs of unfair treatment, understanding the protective laws in place, confidently navigating the complaint process, and tapping into the wealth of support available, you can stand up against discrimination. This not only aids in securing your right to fair housing but also contributes to the broader fight against discrimination, paving the way for a more just and equitable housing landscape for all.

3.8 Pet Policies and Rights

Negotiating a Pet-Friendly Lease

Finding an apartment that meets your needs and welcomes your furry, feathered, or scaled companions can feel like a tall order. Yet, securing a pet-friendly lease is entirely achievable with the right strategy and understanding of pet policies.

Understanding Common Pet Policies

Rental agreements often include specific pet provisions, designed to establish clear guidelines and expectations. Here's what you might encounter.

No Pet Policies

Some properties outright prohibit pets, often due to insurance restrictions or property management preferences.

Breed and Size Restrictions

Even pet-friendly places might have rules about the types of pets allowed. Common restrictions include dog breed limitations, usually targeting larger or "aggressive" breeds, and weight limits.

Number of Pets

There's frequently a cap on how many pets you can have, ensuring the property doesn't become overwhelmed.

Type of Pets

Beyond dogs and cats, policies may specify restrictions on other types of pets, such as reptiles or birds, due to noise, safety, or health concerns. Familiarizing yourself with these policies as you hunt for your next rental can save you time and ensure you're looking at viable options for you and your pets.

Negotiating Pet Terms

When you find a property you love but the pet policy is stricter than you'd hoped, negotiation can sometimes open the door to compromise. Here are some strategies to consider.

Pet Resume

Presenting a pet resume that includes your pet's size, breed, temperament, vaccination records, and references from previous landlords can reassure property managers of your pet's good behavior and your responsibility as an owner.

Meet and Greet

Having the landlord meet your pet can help alleviate concerns about behavior or size, showing that your pet is well-behaved and friendly.

Additional Security Deposit

Proposing an extra security deposit for your pet can cover potential damages, making landlords more amenable to bending their rules.

Pet Rent

While not ideal, agreeing to an additional monthly fee for your pet can sometimes be the key to securing your lease. Approaching negotiations with flexibility and understanding from both sides can lead to a successful agreement that accommodates your pets.

Service and Emotional Support Animals

The landscape changes regarding service animals and emotional support animals (ESAs), as they are not considered pets under the law and are thus not subject to the same restrictions. Here's what you need to know:

Legal Protections

The Americans with Disabilities Act (ADA) and the Fair Housing Act provide protections for individuals with service animals and ESAs, requiring accommodations in housing regardless of pet policies.

Documentation

While not always required, having documentation from a health-care provider that verifies your need for an ESA can help smooth over potential challenges with landlords.

No Extra Fees

Landlords cannot charge pet fees or additional security deposits for service animals or ESAs, recognizing their role in supporting your well-being. Understanding these distinctions and your rights can ensure that your essential companions remain by your side.

Dealing with Pet Deposits and Fees

When pet policies are in place, they often come with associated costs. Here's how to navigate these financial considerations.

Pet Deposits

Separate from your security deposit, pet deposits are specifically to cover any potential damages caused by your pet. These are sometimes refundable, depending on the condition of the rental upon move-out.

Non-refundable Pet Fees

Some landlords charge pet owners a one-time, non-refundable fee. While this can add to your initial moving costs, it's a common practice to cover extra cleaning or maintenance.

Monthly Pet Rent

Increasingly, properties are adding a monthly fee for pet owners to the regular rent. When budgeting for your rental, be sure to factor in this additional cost. While these fees can add up, they are often part of the compromise for living in a rental that welcomes your pets. By budgeting accordingly and understanding the typical costs, you can prepare for these expenses and ensure a happy, harmonious living situation for you and your pets. Navigating the world of pet policies and rights in rental situations requires a blend of preparation, negotiation, and understanding of the law, especially concerning service and emotional support animals. By familiarizing yourself with standard pet policies, employing strategies to negotiate pet-friendly terms, recognizing the legal protections for service and emotional support animals, and understanding the potential financial implications of pet deposits and fees, you can find a rental situation that works for you and your pets. This approach ensures that you're prepared to advocate for your pets and helps build a positive relationship with your landlord, laying the groundwork for a pleasant and stress-free tenancy.

3.9 Safety and Health Regulations in Rentals

Living in a rental unit is not just about making memories in a cozy space; it's also about ensuring that the place you call home doesn't compromise your health or safety. Landlords and tenants have roles to play in maintaining a rental property, but understanding your rights can be your most vital tool in ensuring a safe living environment.

Rights to a Safe Living Environment

Every tenant has the right to live in a space that adheres to local health and safety standards. Landlords must ensure the property is free from hazards that could cause injury or illness. Yet, recognizing what constitutes a safe living environment is

critical.

Structural Integrity

Buildings should be structurally sound, without risk of collapse or falling debris.

Adequate Water and Heating

Tenants are entitled to running water and adequate heating systems, especially during colder months.

Ventilation and Lighting

Proper ventilation helps prevent the buildup of moisture and mold, while adequate lighting contributes to comfort and security.

When these basic needs are unmet, it's crucial to know how to effectively voice your concerns.

Dealing with Health Hazards

Health hazards such as mold, lead paint, and pest infestations diminish the quality of living and pose significant risks to your health. Addressing these issues promptly can prevent minor problems from escalating into significant health risks.

Mold

Often due to excess moisture, mold can lead to respiratory problems. Notify your landlord immediately if you spot signs of mold and request remediation.

Lead Paint

Common in older buildings, lead paint is hazardous, especially to children. A professional inspection can confirm its existence and necessitate removal if you suspect its presence.

Pest Infestations

Landlords are generally responsible for pest control from rodents to insects. Document and report infestations to ensure timely action. Knowing the next steps to take can safeguard your health if these hazards are not addressed.

Safety Features and Requirements

Safety features in rental properties are not just amenities; they are necessities. Smoke detectors, secure locks, and carbon monoxide detectors are essential to your well-being.

Smoke detectors

These are required in all rental units, and they should be tested regularly to ensure they are functioning correctly.

Secure Locks

Doors and windows should have secure locks to protect against unauthorized entry.

Carbon Monoxide Detectors

In properties with gas appliances or attached garages, these detectors are crucial for preventing poisoning from this colorless, odorless gas. Familiarizing yourself with these requirements allows you to assess whether your rental property is up to par and what to do if it falls short.

Legal Recourse for Safety Violations

Legal recourse might be necessary when a rental property fails to meet health and safety standards, and your landlord does not take action despite your reports. The steps to take can vary based on local laws, but a general pathway includes.

Local Housing Authority

Reporting violations to your local housing authority can initiate an inspection and, if necessary, enforcement actions against the landlord.

Rent Escrow

In some jurisdictions, tenants can deposit rent payments into an escrow account instead of paying the landlord directly until repairs are made.

Small Claims Court

Small claims court can be a venue for seeking compensation for unresolved hazards that directly impact your health or lead to personal property damage. Understanding your legal options empowers you to take action when your health and safety are at risk. Maintaining a safe and healthy living environment in a rental property is a shared responsibility, with tenants having the right to demand that safety and health regulations are upheld. Knowing these rights and how to exercise them ensures that your home remains a sanctuary, not just in comfort but also in well-being.

3.10 Legal Resources and Support for Renters

Finding yourself in a situation where you need legal assistance or support regarding rental issues can be daunting. Many renters feel overwhelmed at navigating the complex landscape of tenant laws and rights. However, a wealth of resources is available to guide you through these challenges, ensuring you're not alone in your quest for justice and fairness in your housing situation.

Finding Legal Assistance

When legal issues arise, knowing where to turn for help is crucial. Legal aid organizations offer a lifeline, providing support for various rental issues, from evictions to disputes over repairs. Here's how to connect with these invaluable resources.

Legal Aid Organizations

These groups offer free or low-cost legal services to those who qualify based on income. They can assist with drafting letters to landlords, understanding your lease, and representing you in court if necessary.

Bar Associations

Local bar associations often have referral services connecting you with attorneys specializing in landlord-tenant law. While these services might not be free, they can offer initial consultations at a reduced rate.

University Law Clinics

Some law schools run clinics where law students, supervised by experienced attorneys, provide legal assistance to the community. These clinics can be an excellent resource for renters needing legal help.

Utilizing Tenant Unions and Advocacy Groups

Tenant unions and advocacy groups can be powerful allies. They offer support and advice and champion renters' rights on a broader scale. Joining a tenant union or connecting with an advocacy group can provide several benefits.

Collective Bargaining

Tenant unions often negotiate with landlords on behalf of their members, addressing issues like rent increases and maintenance concerns.

Education and Workshops

Many groups hold workshops that educate renters on their rights and responsibilities, empowering them with knowledge.

Community Support

Being part of a group provides a sense of community and shared purpose, making it easier to navigate challenges.

Educational Resources for

Understanding Your Rights

Knowledge is your best defense when it comes to protecting your rights as a renter. Fortunately, a variety of educational resources are available to help you stay informed:

Online Portals

Websites dedicated to tenant rights are treasure troves of information, offering articles, guides, and FAQs on a wide range of topics.

Books and Publications

Several comprehensive books delve into tenant law, offering insights and advice on navigating rental issues.

Government Resources

HUD and other government agencies provide resources and publications that explain tenant rights and how to seek assistance for housing issues.

Staying Informed About Changes in Tenant Law

Laws and regulations affecting renters are subject to change, so staying informed about these developments is essential. Here are some tips for keeping abreast of the latest updates.

Subscribe to Newsletters

Many legal aid organizations and tenant advocacy groups offer newsletters that highlight recent changes in housing law.

Follow Relevant Blogs and Social Media

Legal experts and tenant rights advocates often share updates and insights through blogs and social media platforms.

Attend Community Meetings

Local housing authorities and tenant unions host meetings where changes in tenant law are discussed. These gatherings can be a good opportunity to learn and ask questions.

Armed with these resources and strategies, you're better equipped to tackle legal challenges related to your rental situation. Whether you're seeking assistance for a specific issue or looking to educate yourself about your rights, a wealth of support is available to guide you through the process.

As we wrap up this exploration of legal resources and support for renters, it's clear that a range of options exists to assist you in navigating the complexities of tenant law. From legal aid organizations that provide direct assistance to tenant unions that offer collective support, to educational materials that empower you with knowledge, these resources play a crucial role in ensuring your rights are protected and your voice is heard. Staying informed and connected with these supports not only strengthens your position as a renter but also contributes to the broader effort to promote fairness and justice in housing.

Moving forward, the journey continues as we delve deeper into the practical aspects of renting. The insights gained from understanding your legal rights and the resources available to support you lay a solid foundation for navigating the challenges and opportunities that lie ahead in the rental landscape.

Chapter 4

Personalizing Your Rental Make it Home Without the Hassle

Transforming a rental into a space that echoes your personality and style might seem like navigating through a maze with restrictions at every turn. The walls may not speak of your journey, and the floors tread the paths of many before you, yet this space is yours to call home, even if the lease says otherwise. Let's tackle the challenge head-on, turning limitations into opportunities for creativity and expression. Here, the focus isn't just on making do but making distinct, personal touches that bring your rental to life, ensuring the place you pay rent for feels every bit the home you dream it to be.

Temporary Touches

Imagine your walls as a blank canvas, albeit one you can't permanently mark. The solution? Removable wallpaper and decals. These wonders of the decorating world empower you to infuse your walls with color, patterns, or even mural-like scenes, all without the commitment or the need for a paintbrush. The beauty of these products lies in their resilience; they stick with you through seasons and moods but part without a trace, leaving walls as pristine as when you first moved in. Whether it's a lush jungle print bringing life to your living room or a geometric pattern adding depth to your study, the transformation is palpable.

Choose designs that reflect your personality

From bold, abstract patterns to soft, serene landscapes.

Consider the room's function and lighting

Lighter colors and delicate patterns can make small spaces feel larger and brighter.

Creative Lighting Solutions

Lighting can make or break the ambiance of a room. It's not just about illuminating spaces; it's about setting the mood, creating comfort zones, and highlighting your home's best features. For renters, the challenge often lies in altering lighting without electrical changes. Enter plug-in sconces, LED strip lights, and smart bulbs. A plug-in sconce beside your bed turns it into a cozy nook for reading, while LED strips under kitchen cabinets add warmth to midnight snack raids. Smart bulbs, which you control from your phone, allow you to adjust colors and brightness to match the time of day or your mood, all without needing a single tool.

Play with color temperatures

Cooler tones for workspaces and warmer lights for relaxation areas.

Layer your lighting

Combine ambient, task, and accent lighting for a dynamic and flexible space.

DIY Furniture and Upcycling

In a world where mass-produced furniture floods our spaces, creating something unique has its charm. Upcycling isn't just about saving items from the landfill; it's a journey into crafting pieces that carry your signature. Start with a simple project: a chair from a thrift store, perhaps, awaiting transformation with a lick of paint or new upholstery. Or, take pallets and reshape them into a rustic coffee table, adding casters for a modern twist. Each project not only results in a piece of furniture but also weaves a story into the fabric of your home. Hunt for potential in second-hand stores, yard sales, and online marketplaces. Gather inspiration from online DIY communities and tutorials, tailoring projects to your skill level and space requirements.

Art Display Without Damage

Art personalizes a space like nothing else, reflecting tastes, inspirations, and dreams. Yet, the dilemma for renters often lies in hanging art without leaving nail holes. The solution is as elegant as the art itself: picture hanging strips, rail systems, and easel stands. These innovations ensure your favorite pieces grace your walls or surfaces without a hammer ever touching a nail. Picture hanging strips, for example, can securely hold frames and are easily removable, leaving no residue or damage. Rail systems, while slightly more involved, offer a way to display multiple pieces with the flexibility to change arrangements as often as you wish.

Map out your gallery wall with paper templates before committing to placement. Mix and match styles, frame sizes, and art types for an eclectic look, or keep it uniform for a cohesive feel. In transforming your rental, the aim is to strike a balance between making it feel indisputably yours and respecting the boundaries set by your lease. With removable wallpaper, your walls tell your stories. Creative lighting options cast your days and nights in the best light, while DIY furniture projects bring a piece of your spirit into every room. And through artful displays, your space becomes a gallery of your adventures, tastes, and dreams. This chapter isn't just about decorating; it's about embedding your identity into the place you live, making it a true reflection of you, all while keeping your security deposit safely intact.

4.2 Maximizing Space in Small Rentals

Living in a snug rental doesn't have to cramp your style or your space. With a bit of ingenuity, you can transform even the tiniest of apartments into a place that feels both spacious and welcoming. Here's how you can cleverly use every inch available, ensuring your rental serves your needs without feeling cluttered.

Furniture That Doubles as Storage

In a small rental, furniture must be more than just functional or aesthetically pleasing; it needs to be a hardworking multitasker.

Opt for pieces that offer additional storage to help keep your space organized and clutter-free. Ottomans with hidden compartments make great places to tuck away blankets or board games, serving as both a footrest and a storage unit. Beds with built-in drawers provide ample space for clothes, spare linens, or out-of-season items, eliminating the need for bulky dressers. Drop-leaf tables can be expanded for dining or workspace needs and folded down to save space when not in use, with storage features for utensils or office supplies. These pieces allow you to maintain a tidy and organized living area, proving that living small doesn't mean sacrificing functionality or style.

Vertical Space Solutions

When floor space is at a premium, look up. The walls and vertical spaces in your rental are prime real estate for storage and decoration. Floating shelves offer a place to store books, display art, or keep kitchen spices within reach without taking up any floor space. Wall-mounted baskets or bins can organize items in the bathroom, kitchen, or entryway, keeping essentials handy but out of the way. Tall narrow shelving units take advantage of vertical space without overwhelming a small room, perfect for storing a variety of items. By thinking vertically, you transform blank walls into functional storage solutions, making your rental feel more spacious and organized.

Illusion of Space

A few strategic choices can trick the eye into perceiving a small rental as more spacious than its square footage suggests. Mirrors placed opposite windows reflect natural light and views, doubling the visual space of a room. A large mirror can act as a statement piece that amplifies light and adds depth. Light colors on walls and large pieces of furniture can make a room feel airier and more open. Soft hues like off-white, light gray, or pastel tones are your allies in creating the illusion of space. Multi-functional furniture like a nesting table set can be tucked away when not in use, reducing visual clutter and opening up the floor space. Implementing these strategies helps to create a sense of openness, ensuring your rental feels welcoming and less confined.

Decluttering Strategies

Embracing a minimalist approach to your possessions is not just about aesthetics; it's a practical strategy for maximizing the utility of a small space. Regular purges keep clutter at bay. Every few months, take stock of your belongings and decide what really serves you. If it hasn't been used in the last year and doesn't bring you joy, it might be time to let it go. Digital solutions for physical clutter can be a game-changer. Opt for digital subscriptions or streaming services instead of physical copies of books, magazines, or DVDs. Vertical storage solutions not only make use of unused space but also encourage you to keep only what fits comfortably in your designated storage areas, preventing accumulation of unnecessary items. By regularly assessing and organizing your belongings, you ensure your living space remains functional and clutter-free, making your small rental feel more like a carefully curated haven. Living in a small rental presents unique challenges, but with the right strategies, it can also offer unique opportunities for creativity and organization. By choosing furniture that doubles as storage, making use of vertical space, creating the illusion of more space, and adopting decluttering strategies, you can transform your compact living situation into a comfortable, stylish home that meets your needs and reflects your personal style, all while keeping clutter at bay.

4.3 Sustainable Living in a Rental

Living sustainably in a rental space might seem like a daunting task at first glance. The restrictions of a lease can often feel like barriers to implementing larger green initiatives. However, with a few smart adjustments and a dash of creativity, renters can significantly reduce their environmental impact, even within the confines of a leased property. Let's explore how you can incorporate sustainability into your rental, from energy-saving hacks and water conservation methods to embracing eco-friendly products and waste reduction practices.

Energy Efficiency Hacks

Reducing energy consumption in your rental not only contributes to a healthier planet but can also lead to lower utility bills. Here are some effective strategies. Switch to LED Bulbs, these consume up to 75% less energy than traditional incandescent bulbs and last much longer, making them a win–win for both your wallet and the environment. Smart Power Strips stop phantom energy drains from devices that remain plugged in and can add up. Smart power strips cut power to devices when they're not in use, tackling energy waste effortlessly. Thermal Curtains insulate your windows witch can help regulate indoor temperatures, reducing the need for heating in winter and air conditioning in summer. Energy-Efficient Appliances, If you're in a position to choose or influence the selection of appliances in your rental, opt for those with high Energy Star ratings. By integrating these simple changes, you can significantly contribute to energy conservation in your rental without needing to overhaul the property's infrastructure.

Eco-Friendly Products

Every product we purchase has an environmental footprint, from its production and packaging to its disposal. Making mindful choices about the products we bring into our rental homes can have a profound impact. Biodegradable Cleaning Products, Opt for cleaning agents made from natural, biodegradable ingredients that are kind to the planet and your indoor air quality. Reusable Personal Items, ditch single-use plastics in favor of reusable water bottles, coffee cups, and shopping bags. Even small changes like using bar soap instead of plastic-bottled body wash can make a difference. Sustainable Kitchenware, choose bamboo or wooden cooking utensils and biodegradable dishcloths over plastic alternatives. Second-Hand and Upcycled Items, embrace pre-loved furniture and decor to reduce demand for new, resource-intensive products. Incorporating these products into your daily life supports a sustainable lifestyle and sets a precedent for eco-conscious living, even within a rental.

Water Conservation

Water is a precious resource, and conserving it is crucial for sustainable living. Renters can implement several strategies to minimize water usage. Low-Flow Showerheads, these fixtures reduce water flow without compromising pressure, dramatically reducing water usage during showers. Faucet Aerators, installing aerators on your taps mixes air with water, reducing water use while maintaining water pressure. Efficient Dishwashing, fill the sink rather than letting the water run when hand-washing dishes, and only run the dishwasher when it's full. Fix Leaks Promptly, a dripping faucet can waste a surprising amount of water over time. Report and fix any leaks as soon as they're noticed. These water-saving techniques are not only beneficial for the environment but can also lead to reduced utility bills, making them advantageous for both renters and the planet.

Recycling and Composting in Limited Spaces

Effective waste management is a cornerstone of sustainable living, and even renters with limited space can make a significant contribution to reducing landfill waste. Recycling Stations, set up a small recycling station in your home to separate paper, plastics, metals, and glass. Many municipalities offer recycling pickup services or have drop-off locations. Composting, if you have a balcony or small outdoor area, consider a compact compost bin for food scraps. For those without outdoor space, worm composting systems or bokashi bins can fit under a sink and don't produce odors. Digital Subscriptions, reduce paper waste by opting for digital versions of magazines, bills, and newspapers. Reusable Containers minimize packaging waste by using reusable containers for food storage and shopping. Adopting these recycling and composting practices can dramatically reduce the amount of waste you send to the landfill, making your rental a key player in your sustainable lifestyle. Implementing sustainable practices in a rental doesn't require grand gestures or complete overhauls of your living space. Through mindful choices in energy consumption, product selection, water usage, and waste management, renters can make a significant environmental impact. These adjustments not only contribute to a healthier planet but also foster a sense of responsibility and stewardship for the environment, proving that sustainable living is achievable, even within the constraints of a rental agreement.

4.4 Smart Home Gadgets for Renters

In the age where technology infuses every aspect of our lives, making your rental smarter with gadgets that require zero installation is not just a possibility; it's a game-changer. These innovations offer both convenience and a layer of security, enhancing your rental life without risking your deposit. Let us explore how you can elevate your rental with smart home devices designed for the modern tenant.

Non-Permanent Smart Home Devices

The beauty of non-permanent smart gadgets lies in their simplicity and impact. Devices such as smart bulbs and plugs transform everyday appliances into intelligent companions with minimal effort. Smart bulbs can be controlled remotely, changing the ambiance of your space with adjustable colors and brightness levels. Imagine setting a wake-up routine with lights that gradually brighten, mimicking sunrise inside your bedroom. Smart plugs turn any regular appliance into a smart device. With a plug and a smartphone app, you can control your coffee maker, lamp, or fan from anywhere, ensuring you never return to a dark home or leave devices running unnecessarily. These gadgets are not only about adding convenience but also about energy conservation and enhancing your rental's functionality without permanent changes.

Enhancing Security

Security in a rental can feel limited, given the restrictions on installations. Yet, wireless technology brings robust security options that respect your lease terms. Wireless security cameras, easily mounted with adhesive strips or stands, offer peace of mind by monitoring your home in real-time. Look for cameras with two-way audio, motion detection, and night vision to keep an eye on your space, pets, or to verify visitors without altering the property. Smart locks present a keyless way to secure your rental. Models that fit over existing deadbolts allow you to lock and unlock your door with a smartphone, generate temporary codes for guests, and track access without replacing the lock itself. With these devices, enhancing your rental's security becomes an effortless task that leaves no trace once you move out.

Smart Thermostats for Renters

Adapting your living environment to your schedule and preferences while saving on energy bills becomes a reality with smart thermostats. Although you may not be able to replace the existing thermostat permanently, portable options exist that work with existing systems and offer the ability to adjust temperatures from anywhere, ensuring your home is always the perfect temperature when you arrive and conserving energy when you're away. Learning capabilities that adapt to your schedule and preferences over time, optimizing energy usage without constant manual adjustments. While some landlords might be hesitant, presenting the benefits of reduced energy costs and offering to revert to the original setup upon moving out can make the case for adding a smart thermostat to your rental.

Voice-Activated Convenience

The integration of voice assistants into your rental introduces a level of convenience previously unimagined. Devices like Amazon Echo Dot or Google Nest Mini require no installation and become central hubs for controlling your smart home devices through voice commands. Start your day with a custom routine where a simple "Good morning" command turns on your lights, reads out the day's weather, and starts brewing your coffee. Control entertainment systems, set reminders, or manage your shopping list all through voice commands, making your rental not just a living space but a responsive environment that adapts to your needs. The transition to smart living in a rental doesn't necessitate complex installations or alterations. Through non-permanent smart home devices, enhanced security options, adaptable smart thermostats, and the convenience of voice-activated assistants, you can enjoy the benefits of a connected home. These advancements allow you to personalize and secure your space, providing comfort, convenience, and a touch of modernity, all while keeping your rental agreement intact.

4.5 Cultivating a Home Garden

in Limited Spaces

In the realms of concrete and compact living, the dream of nurturing a garden often seems far-fetched. Yet, with a sprinkle of creativity and a dash of determination, the seemingly impossible becomes possible, transforming your rental into a green oasis. This section unfolds the secrets to thriving indoor and balcony gardens, ventures into the innovative world of hydroponics, and celebrates the communal spirit of community gardening. Each segment not only brings you closer to nature but also enhances your living space, improving air quality and adding a touch of vitality.

Indoor Gardening

Creating a lush indoor garden in a rental meshes the beauty of nature with the coziness of home. Here's how to start, select the right plants, opt for species that thrive indoors, such as snake plants, pothos, or spider plants, known for their low maintenance and air-purifying qualities. Light it Right, position plants near windows but beware of direct sunlight, which might be too harsh for some. Supplement with grow lights if natural light is scarce. Mind the Water, overwatering is a common misstep. Ensure pots have drainage and water only when the topsoil feels dry. Fertilize Thoughtfully, a gentle, organic fertilizer every few months keeps your indoor garden vibrant without overwhelming your plants or your living space with chemicals. Each plant becomes a living decor element, contributing to a serene and inviting atmosphere in your rental. Balcony and Window Gardening For those with balconies or generous window sills, the extension of green space becomes a tangible reality. Here's how to maximize these areas, Container Gardening, use pots and planters that fit your space. Consider vertical planters or hanging pots to utilize vertical space efficiently. Choose Suitable Plants, hardy herbs like rosemary and thyme, compact vegetables like cherry tomatoes, or flowering plants such as petunias thrive in balcony conditions. Regulate Sunlight, use plant stands or movable containers to manage sun exposure, ensuring your plants get just the right amount of light. protect from elements. Be prepared to move plants indoors during extreme weather or use protective covers to shield them from harsh conditions. This approach not only beautifies your rental's exterior but also allows you to grow your own herbs or vegetables, adding freshness to your meals and satisfaction to your gardening endeavors.

Hydroponics for Beginners

Hydroponics, the art of growing plants in water without soil, suits the rental lifestyle perfectly, offering a clean, efficient, and surprisingly simple method of gardening. Here's how to dive in. Start with a Kit numerous hydroponic kits are available for beginners, providing all you need to start your soil-less garden.

Select Appropriate Plants

Leafy greens like lettuce and herbs such as basil adapt well to hydroponic systems and are ideal for first-time gardeners. Monitor Water and Nutrients, regularly check water levels and nutrient mixtures to ensure your plants are well-fed and hydrated. Enjoy the Harvest, hydroponic systems can produce bountiful harvests in small spaces, rewarding you with fresh produce right from your window or balcony. Hydroponics introduces you to a futuristic way of gardening, minimizing mess and maximizing yield, a perfect harmony for renters.

Community Gardening

Sometimes, the desire to dig in the dirt and connect with a larger patch of earth calls for stepping outside your rental. Community gardens offer a splendid opportunity to cultivate not just plants but also relationships. Here's your pathway to participation. Find a Local Garden, search for community gardens in your area or inquire at local gardening clubs or municipal offices. Understand the Commitment, each garden has its guidelines and expectations. Some might require a small fee or specific hours of participation. Learn and Contribute, community gardens are excellent places to learn from experienced gardeners. Offer your time, learn from others, and enjoy the communal harvest. engage with your community beyond gardening, these spaces often host workshops, social events, and educational programs, enriching your connection to the local community. Engaging in community gardening extends your living space beyond the confines of your rental, offering fresh air, camaraderie, and the joy of collective gardening efforts. In transforming your rental into a haven of greenery, from the tranquility of indoor plants and the charm of balcony gardens to the innovative venture into hydroponics and the communal spirit of community gardens, you invite nature into your urban living space. Each plant nurtured, each seed sown, not only beautifies your rental but also connects you deeply with the rhythms of nature, offering a serene escape and a sense of accomplishment in the heart of the city.

4.6 Community Engagement: Making Connections in Your Area

Creating a sense of belonging in a new area, especially as a renter, presents its own unique set of challenges and opportunities. The first step often involves venturing beyond the four walls of your rental and diving into the vibrant tapestry of your local community. This exploration not only enriches your personal life but also weaves a network of connections that can transform any place into home.

Local Events and Groups

Every community has a heartbeat, a rhythm created by its events, clubs, and groups that bring people together. Identifying these gatherings requires a bit of curiosity and exploration. Local Bulletin Boards and Cafés, often, these are goldmines for community events, from art shows to book clubs, that invite locals to connect and share experiences. Community Centers and Libraries, these institutions regularly host workshops, classes, and events catering to a wide range of interests and ages, offering a nurturing environment to learn new skills and meet neighbors. Farmers' Markets and Festivals, these gatherings are not only about shopping local but also about celebrating the community's culture, where conversations start easily and friendships take root. Participating actively in these local happenings allows you to blend into the fabric of your community, making meaningful connections while supporting local initiatives.

Neighborhood Apps and Online Communities

Connecting with your neighborhood has never been easier in today's digital ager. Several apps and online platforms provide spaces for residents to share news, recommendations, and even warnings about local issues. Next-door, a neighborhood hub for trusted connections where you can get to know your neighbors, exchange local advice, and assist one another. Meetup, whether you're looking for hiking buddies or fellow book enthusiasts, Meetup helps you join groups with shared interests in your vicinity. Facebook Groups. Many communities have dedicated Facebook groups where members post about events, services, and community concerns. These digital tools act as bridges, linking you to your neighborhood's pulse, ensuring you're always just a click away from the next local gathering or urgent community update.

Volunteering Opportunities

Giving back to the community not only fosters a sense of belonging but also roots you deeply in the local culture and its well-being. Volunteering can take various forms, depending on your interests and the community's needs. Community Gardens, lend a hand in beautifying communal spaces, where the fruits of your labor benefit the whole neighborhood. Local Nonprofits and Charities. These organizations always need extra hands, whether for organizing events, running campaigns, or helping out in daily operations. School and Library Programs, offering your time and skills can greatly support educational programs, tutoring sessions, and after-school activities. The act of volunteering places you at the heart of community improvement efforts, creating a sense of pride and connection to the place you call home.

Creating Social Spaces

Sometimes, building community connections means taking the initiative to create gathering opportunities. This can be especially rewarding, as it allows you to tailor social interactions to your interests. Potluck Dinners and Game Nights, invite neighbors for a casual evening of food, games, and conversation. These gatherings provide a relaxed setting to deepen connections. Skill-Sharing Workshops, if you have a particular skill, like knitting, photography, or coding, organize a small workshop for interested neighbors. It's a great way to share knowledge and discover common interests. Book and Film Clubs, starting a club around books or films can lead to stimulating discussions and shared experiences, cementing friendships and fostering a sense of community. Taking the lead in organizing such events not only positions you as an active community member but also brings the joy of shared experiences and mutual discovery.

Engaging with your community through local events, digital platforms, volunteering, and creating social spaces lays down roots that transform a living space into a home. It turns neighbors into friends and unfamiliar streets into familiar haunts. This engagement enriches your rental experience, making it more than just a temporary spot on your life's journey but a vibrant chapter filled with connections and memories.

4.7 Dealing with Difficult Neighbors: A Peaceful Approach

Living closely with others brings about its own set of challenges, not least among them the occasional difficult neighbor. Whether it's late-night noise, encroaching pets, or just a lack of common courtesy, these situations require a delicate touch and a strategy aimed at peaceful coexistence. Here's how to maintain harmony, or at least a respectful understanding, in close quarters living.

Effective Communication

Opening lines of dialogue with neighbors who might be causing discomfort is often the first and most crucial step towards resolution. It's easy for small irritations to fester into major grievances if left unaddressed, but how you approach these conversations can make all the difference. Choose the Right Moment, approach your neighbor at a time that's calm and convenient for both of you, avoiding times when tensions might already be high. Be Clear and Kind when explaining the issue, focus on how the situation affects you rather than accusing them of wrongdoing. Use "I" statements to express your feelings and needs. Offer Solutions. Rather than just presenting a problem, suggest practical solutions or compromises that could work for both parties. This approach not only shows respect for your neighbor's perspective but also makes it clear that you're seeking a solution that respects the needs and comforts of everyone involved.

Understanding Noise Ordinances

Noise is a common source of friction between neighbors, especially in densely populated living environments. Being aware of local noise ordinances gives you a solid foundation for discussions

about noise levels and can help ensure that any complaints or requests you make are grounded in shared legal standards. Research
Local Laws, familiarize yourself with the specific noise regulations
in your area, which often define acceptable noise levels by time
of day. Share Knowledge, if noise is an issue, gently inform your
neighbor about these ordinances, as they may not be aware of the
specific rules. Document Disturbances, keeping a log of noise disturbances, including times and dates, can be useful if the situation
escalates and requires mediation or official intervention. Armed
with this knowledge, you can approach conversations about noise
from an informed standpoint, making it clear that your concerns
are based on shared community standards rather than personal
preference.

Seeking Mediation

When direct communication doesn't lead to a resolution, or if the
thought of face-to-face conversations is too daunting, third-party
mediation can be an invaluable tool. Mediators offer a neutral
perspective, helping both parties feel heard and working towards a
mutually acceptable solution. Find a Local Mediator, many communities offer free or low-cost mediation services through local
government or nonprofit organizations. Prepare for the Session,
before mediation, outline the points you want to address and think
about possible compromises you'd be willing to make. Engage
in the Process, approach mediation with an open mind, ready
to listen to your neighbor's perspective and work collaboratively
towards a solution. This process can not only help resolve the
immediate issue but also lay the groundwork for more positive
interactions in the future.

Maintaining Privacy

In close living situations, maintaining a sense of privacy can
sometimes be as challenging as dealing with noise or other dis-

turbances. Here are some strategies to enhance your privacy and comfort. Use Window Treatments, curtains, blinds, or privacy film can prevent neighbors from looking into your home without blocking natural light. Create Natural Barriers, plants, either in containers or as a vertical garden, can offer privacy on balconies or patios while adding a touch of greenery. Soundproof Your Space, adding rugs, wall hangings, or bookshelves can help absorb sound, minimizing how much of your life is audible to neighbors. By taking steps to enhance your privacy, you create a more comfortable and personal space within your rental, reducing the potential for overexposure to neighbors and fostering a sense of personal sanctuary.

Navigating the complexities of neighborly coexistence requires patience, empathy, and sometimes a bit of creativity. From initiating a conversation with a clear and kind approach, understanding the local laws that govern communal living, seeking out third-party mediation to bridge stubborn divides, to taking practical steps to enhance your personal privacy, these strategies serve as a roadmap for dealing with difficult neighbors. Each action taken is a step towards fostering a peaceful, respectful community where everyone can feel at home, valued, and understood.

4.8 Renewing Your Space: Low-Cost Redecorating Ideas

In the ever-evolving landscape of our lives, our homes serve as the backdrop to countless memories and milestones. Yet, over time, the once exciting and fresh aura of our rental spaces can fade into the background, becoming all too familiar. The quest for rejuvenation need not be a call to overhaul everything within your four walls but rather an opportunity to breathe new life into your space with thoughtful, low-cost redecorating ideas. It's about seeing the potential in the everyday, transforming the mundane into the extraordinary with a few simple changes.

Seasonal Updates

With the changing seasons comes a natural desire to refresh our surroundings, mirroring the transition happening outdoors. This doesn't necessarily mean a complete decor overhaul with each season but rather introducing subtle accents and elements that nod to the time of year. Cushions and Throws, swap out cushion covers and throws to reflect seasonal colors or themes. Light, airy fabrics in spring and summe and warm, textured materials for fall and winter, can dramatically alter the mood of a room. Seasonal Decor, a vase of spring blooms, a bowl of summer fruits, autumn leaves in glass jars, or a string of fairy lights in winter can all serve as simple yet effective nods to the season. Scented Candles and Diffusers, scents have the power to evoke seasons. Citrus or floral scents for warmer months and woodsy, spiced aromas for the colder part of the year can subtly transform the ambiance of your space.

Rearranging for a New Perspective

Sometimes, all it takes to refresh your rental is to view it from a different angle. Rearranging furniture can significantly impact the look and feel of your space, often without spending a dime. Create a New Focal Point, Shift the orientation of your living room from the TV to a striking piece of art or a beautiful window view. Flow and Functionality, consider the flow of movement through your space. Reconfiguring furniture to eliminate bottlenecks can make your home feel more spacious and open. Zone Your Space, use rugs, shelving units, or even the arrangement of furniture to create distinct zones for different activities, giving your rental a sense of variety and purpose.

DIY Projects

Embracing DIY projects not only allows for a personalized touch to your decor but also for a sense of achievement and creativity. Simple projects can have a significant impact, transforming the look and feel of your rental on a budget. Paint an Accent Wall, if your lease permits, a fresh coat of paint on a single wall can serve as a vibrant backdrop or a subtle hint of color. Update Hardware, changing out dated or dull hardware on cabinets and doors can instantly modernize a space. Recover and Repurpose, give old furniture a new lease on life with a bit of fabric and some staple guns or transform crates into rustic shelving.

Thrift and Antique Finds

Treasure hunting in thrift stores and antique markets can yield unique pieces that add character and charm to your rental. These finds not only tell a story but also prevent the need for new productions, aligning with a sustainable approach to decorating.

Mix and Match

Don't be afraid to mix periods and styles. A sleek modern lamp on an ornate vintage table can create an intriguing juxtaposition. Restore and Refinish, look beyond surface imperfections. A bit of sanding and a coat of paint can reveal the beauty beneath. Personalize, use your thrifted finds as a base for personalization. Decoupage, fabric wraps, or simply a new set of knobs can transform your find into something uniquely yours. In navigating the creative process of renewing your space, remember that the most impactful changes often stem from a place of intention and imagination. Whether it's aligning your decor with the seasons, shifting perspectives through rearrangement, diving into DIY projects, or discovering the potential in thrifted treasures, the journey to revitalizing your rental is one of exploration and experimentation. It's about allowing your space to evolve with you, reflecting your journey, your tastes, and your aspirations. Through these low-cost redecorating ideas, your rental becomes more than just a temporary dwelling; it transforms into a dynamic canvas that celebrates change, creativity, and the comfort of home.

4.9 Hosting in a Rental: Tips for Small Spaces

When you're living in a rental, especially one with limited square footage, hosting friends and family might seem like a puzzle. However, with some clever adjustments and a touch of creativity, your cozy space can become the perfect spot for memorable gatherings. From furniture that adapts to your needs to creating the perfect atmosphere, let's explore how to make the most of your small rental for entertaining.

Space-Saving Furniture

The right furniture can transform a tight space into a versatile entertaining area. Investing in pieces that serve dual purposes or can be easily stored away when not in use ensures your rental remains functional and spacious. Nesting Tables, these can be spread out to provide multiple surfaces for drinks and snacks during a gathering and then tucked away into a compact form. Fold-Down Desks and Tables, mounted on the wall, these can serve as a buffet or bar area for your event and fold back up to reclaim floor space afterward. Stackable Stools and Chairs, easy to store and quick to set up, stackable seating options ensure everyone has a place without cluttering your living area. With these adaptable furniture choices, you can swiftly shift from everyday living to host mode, ensuring your guests are comfortable without your space feeling cramped.

Creative Seating Solutions

When the guest list outnumbers your seating arrangements, it's time to get creative. There are numerous ways to offer everyone a spot without resorting to standing room only. Floor Cushions and Poufs, these are not only trendy but also incredibly practical. Scatter a few around your coffee table for a casual and comfy seating option. Window Sills, with a few cushions, wider window sills can become cozy perches for guests to sit and chat. Ottomans, often used as footrests or coffee tables, ottomans can double as extra seating. Choose ones that are sturdy and flat-topped for versatility. These innovative solutions not only maximize your available seating but also foster a casual, intimate atmosphere, encouraging guests to mingle and relax.

Ambiance and Mood

The atmosphere of your gathering can leave a lasting impression on your guests, turning even the smallest of spaces into a warm and inviting setting. Here are some tips to enhance the ambiance of your rental. Lighting , soft warm lighting instantly makes a space feel welcoming. Use lamps with dimmable options or string lights to create a gentle glow that flatters your space and your guests. Music, a carefully curated playlist can set the tone for the evening. Keep the volume at a level that encourages conversation, opting for genres that complement the mood you wish to create. Decor, a few well-placed decorations can elevate your space. Consider fresh flowers in mason jars or unique, thrifted pieces that spark conversation. Creating the right atmosphere is about engaging the senses, making your guests feel comfortable and cherished from the moment they step into your home.

Simplifying Food and Drinks

When space is limited, simplifying your menu and how it's served can make hosting much easier. Here are some ideas for keeping the culinary aspect of your gathering both impressive and manageable. Buffet Style, set up a buffet on your kitchen counter or a fold-down table. This encourages guests to serve themselves, saving space and reducing the need for a large dining table. Finger Foods, Opt for appetizers and small bites that don't require cutlery. This not only simplifies eating in a small space but also minimizes cleanup. Signature Drink, instead of stocking a full bar, offer a signature cocktail or mocktail that can be pre-mixed in a large pitcher. Add a selection of beers, wines, and non-alcoholic options to round out your offerings. By focusing on simplicity and self-service, you can provide a delightful culinary experience that allows you to enjoy the company of your guests without the constant need to manage or serve.

Hosting in a small rental presents unique challenges, but with the right approach, it can be an enjoyable and fulfilling experience. Space-saving furniture ensures your home remains adaptable, creative seating solutions provide comfort for your guests, and the right ambiance and mood set the stage for a memorable gathering. Simplifying food and drinks further ensures that your event is not only manageable but also leaves your guests impressed with your hosting skills. With these strategies, your small rental can become the perfect venue for gatherings that are big on warmth, charm, and connection.

4.10 Moving Out: Leaving Your Rental Better Than You Found It

When the time comes to pack up and move on, leaving your rental in pristine condition reflects not just on your respect for the space but also on your integrity as a tenant. This part of your rental journey should be approached with as much care and attention as when you first moved in. Here's how to ensure you leave your rental spotlessly, possibly even in better shape than you found it, paving the way for a smooth transition and securing your security deposit.

Cleaning and Repair Checklist

A meticulous cleaning and repair effort can transform the look of your rental, returning it to its original state or better. Tackling one room at a time ensures no nook or cranny is overlooked. Dust and wash all surfaces, including countertops, shelves, and fixtures. Deep clean the bathroom and kitchen, paying extra attention to appliances, which should be left spotless inside and out. Repair any minor damage such as holes from hanging pictures or scuffs on the walls. Matching paint can usually be obtained for touch-ups if you saved the details or can find out from your landlord. Carpets should be vacuumed and shampooed if necessary, especially if pets were in the home. This thorough approach not only demonstrates your respect for the property but also minimizes the likelihood of charges being deducted from your security deposit for cleaning or repairs.

Organizing Your Move

A smooth move requires organization and planning. Starting early and categorizing your belongings can make the process far less stressful. Begin packing non-essential items weeks in advance, clearly labeling each box with its contents and intended room. Create an inventory of your belongings to keep track of what you have and to ensure nothing is left behind. If hiring movers, research and book early to get the best rates and ensure availability on your desired date. Prepare an essentials box for your first night in your new place, including toiletries, a change of clothes, and any immediate necessities. Strategically managing the logistics of your move helps prevent last-minute chaos, ensuring a calm and collected relocation.

Restoring Original Features

Some personalizations you've made to your rental might need to be undone before your departure. This step is crucial for adhering to the terms of your lease and leaving the property in its original condition. Remove any hardware or fixtures you've added, replacing them with the originals if you still have them. If you've painted, revert the wall colors back to their original state, assuming this was a condition of your lease. Take down any window treatments that weren't provided with the rental, ensuringthe property's original items are stored safely for reinstallationy. This attention to detail shows a deep respect for the landlord's property and can positively influence the final inspection.

Securing Your Security Deposit

The return of your full security deposit is often contingent on the condition in which you leave the rental. To ensure you've done everything possible, document the property's condition with photos or a video after you've completed your cleaning and repairs. This can provide evidence if there's a dispute over its condition. Inform your landlord or property manager in writing of your intended move-out date and request a final walk-through. This gives you a chance to address any concerns they might have on the spot. Provide your forwarding address where the security deposit can be sent, and inquire about the expected timeline for its return. Taking these steps fosters a transparent and proactive exit process, setting a positive tone for the final interactions with your landlord or property manager. In wrapping up your time in your rental, a thoughtful and thorough approach to moving out—not just in packing your belongings but in caring for the space itself—can leave a lasting positive impression. From a detailed clean and repair regimen to careful planning of the move itself, and from restoring the original character of the home to ensuring the security deposit is returned, these steps are about honoring the space that has been your home. As we shift focus, remember that the care and attention you give to leaving well not only secures your financial investment but also solidifies a respectful and responsible tenant reputation, easing the way into your next adventure.

Chapter 5

Navigating the Rental Markets

Imagine walking into a bustling market, the air buzzing with energy, vendors calling out the day's specials, and the smell of fresh produce in the air. Now, replace the stalls with listings, the vendors with landlords and property managers, and the goods with apartments and houses. This is the rental market – dynamic, ever-changing, and full of opportunities if you know where to look. Understanding this market, with its highs and lows, seasonal shifts, and hidden gems, is crucial for anyone looking to find a great deal on their next rental.

In this chapter, we're going to break down the key trends and patterns that shape the rental market, equipping you with the knowledge to navigate these waters with confidence. From understanding how market fluctuations can impact your rent, to knowing when and where to look for the best deals, we're covering all the bases. Plus, we'll look ahead, exploring how to read the signs of what's to come in the rental landscape.

Analyzing Market Fluctuations

The rental market, much like the stock market, is influenced by a variety of factors - economic conditions, supply and demand, and even seasonal changes. Prices can swing, availability can vary, and knowing how to read these trends can give you an edge.

Supply and Demand

When more people are looking to rent than there are properties available, prices go up. Conversely, if there are lots of vacancies, landlords might offer deals to attract tenants. Economic Conditions, in booming economic times, people might be able to afford more, driving rents up. In tougher times, the opposite can occur.

Local Events and Developments

A new university opening, a tech company expanding into the area, or major construction projects can all impact rental prices and availability. Keeping an eye on local news, economic reports, and even community bulletin boards can provide valuable insights into how these factors are playing out in your area.

Seasonal Considerations in Renting

Timing is everything, and believe it or not, there are peak and off-peak seasons for renting. Generally, the summer months see a surge in rental activity. Families prefer to move when school is out, and warmer weather makes for easier moving conditions. However, this increased demand can drive prices up. On the flip side, winter months typically see a slowdown in the rental market.

Fewer people are looking to move, which means landlords might be more willing to negotiate to fill vacancies.

Best Time to Rent

Late fall through winter. You might find lower prices and more willing negotiators. When to Start Looking, if you're aiming for a summer move, start your search early in the spring to get ahead of the competition.

Emerging Neighborhoods

Every city has its hit parade of popular neighborhood that everyone flocks to, driving rents up. But the savvy renter looks to the up-and-comers, areas that might not be on everyone's radar yet but are on the brink of becoming the next big thing. Signs of an Up-and-Coming Area, new small businesses opening up, improvement in public transportation, and renovations in public spaces. Why Consider These Areas, not only can you get in at a lower rent before prices rise, but you might also enjoy watching a neighborhood come into its own. Researching, talking to locals, and even spending some time exploring these areas can uncover some hidden gems.

Future Predictions

Staying one step ahead requires a bit of foresight. While no one has a crystal ball, certain indicators can hint at where the rental market is headed. Development Plans, keep an eye on city or neighborhood development plans. An influx of new housing can shift the market. Economic Forecasts, general economic trends can also provide clues. A strong job market might mean a more competitive rental market is on the horizon. Historical Data, looking at how rents have changed in the past during similar conditions can offer a window into future trends. While predicting the future is never a certainty, being informed can help you make smarter decisions about when and where to rent. Navigating the rental market's waves doesn't have to feel like a daunting task. With a bit of knowledge about how market dynamics work, an understanding of the best times to rent, an eye for emerging neighborhoods, and a forward-looking approach, you can find yourself well-positioned to catch the best deals. Remember, every renter's situation is unique, and what works for one might not work for another. But armed with these insights, you're better equipped to find a rental that fits not just your budget, but your life too.

5.2 The Art of Rental Arbitrage

Rental arbitrage might sound complex, but at its core, it's a straightforward strategy. This approach involves renting a property and then re-renting it on a short-term basis, essentially turning a long-term lease into a profitable venture. The difference between the rent you pay and what you earn from short-term rentals is your profit. It's a method that has gained traction, offering individuals a way to enter the real estate market without the hefty initial investment of buying a property.

Rental Arbitrage Explained

At first glance, rental arbitrage seems like a win-win. You don't need to own real estate to start earning from it. Instead, you lease a property under clear terms that allow for subletting or short-term rentals and then list it on platforms like Airbnb or VRBO. The key here is finding the right property in a desirable location where short-term demand is high. Urban centers, tourist spots, or areas near major events and businesses can be goldmines for arbitrage opportunities.

Legal and Ethical Considerations

Before diving into rental arbitrage, it's crucial to navigate the legal landscape. Not all leases permit subletting, and some cities have regulations around short-term rentals.

Lease Agreements

Review your lease agreement carefully or negotiate terms that allow for subletting. Being transparent with your landlord about your intentions can prevent future conflicts.

Local Laws

Many cities have implemented regulations that affect short-term rentals, including limitations on the number of days a property can be rented out annually and the need for specific licenses. Ensure you're fully compliant to avoid fines or legal issues.

Ethical Considerations

Consider the impact on the neighborhood. Maintaining a good relationship with neighbors and ensuring your guests respect local norms is vital for the long-term success of your arbitrage venture.

Success Stories

Learning from those who have succeeded in rental arbitrage can provide valuable insights. For instance, a case study might detail an individual who leased several apartments in a city popular for its festivals and conferences. By furnishing these apartments tastefully and marketing them effectively, they managed to secure a steady stream of short-term tenants, significantly increasing their monthly income. However, these case studies also highlight common pitfalls, such as underestimating the costs of furnishing and maintaining properties or failing to account for occupancy fluctuations.

Getting Started

Launching your own rental arbitrage endeavor requires careful planning and execution. Here are practical steps to get you started:

Budgeting

Start with a clear budget that covers the lease, furnishing, utilities, insurance, and marketing costs. Don't forget to set aside a contingency fund for unexpected expenses.

Finding the Right Property

Look for properties in high-demand areas where short-term rentals are allowed. Consider factors such as proximity to attractions, accessibility, and the overall appeal of the neighborhood.

Setting Up Your Rental

Furnish and decorate your rental to appeal to a broad audience. High-quality photos and detailed, honest descriptions are critical for your online listings.

Managing Your Rentals

Decide whether you'll manage your rental yourself or use a property management service. Self-management can increase profits but requires time and dedication, especially for guest communication and property maintenance. Rental arbitrage opens up a path to generating income from real estate without the need to purchase property. With the right approach, attention to legal details, and dedication to providing a great experience for your guests, it can be a rewarding venture. Remember, success in rental arbitrage doesn't just come from filling up your calendar but from creating memorable stays that lead to positive reviews, repeat business, and steady income growth.

5.3 Building a Positive Relationship

with Your Landlord

A harmonious rapport with your landlord isn't just a bonus—it's a key element of a stress-free rental experience. This relationship, based on mutual respect and understanding, can transform your rental into a place you're excited to call home. Let's explore how open communication, empathy for your landlord's perspective, savvy negotiation for upgrades, and the perks of being a long-term tenant can contribute to a beneficial partnership for both parties.

Open Communication

Keeping the lines of communication transparent and proactive is vital. Here are some strategies to maintain a positive dialogue. Initiate Early Conversations, reach out to introduce yourself shortly after moving in. A simple gesture like this sets a cooperative tone. Regular Updates, if a maintenance issue arises or you'll be away for an extended period, inform your landlord promptly. Keeping them in the loop shows respect for their property and can prevent minor issues from escalating. Respectful Feedback, should you have concerns or suggestions, present them politely and constructively. Framing feedback as a benefit to both you and the landlord can lead to more productive discussions. Through consistent and considerate communication, you lay the groundwork for a relationship built on trust and mutual respect, making it easier to navigate any challenges that arise.

Understanding Landlord Perspectives

To foster a positive relationship, it's helpful to see things from your landlord's point of view. Recognizing their concerns can open the door to solutions that benefit both of you. Property Care, landlords value tenants who treat the property with respect. Simple actions like regular cleaning and promptly reporting issues demonstrate your commitment. Reliability, consistent on-time rent payments are a landlord's top priority. If you anticipate a delay, inform your landlord as soon as possible and propose a solution. Open to Improvements. Many landlords are open to making reasonable upgrades that enhance the property's value and your quality of life. Showing that you care about the property's condition can encourage them to invest in improvements. By understanding and addressing your landlord's priorities, you can create a cooperative environment that encourages them to be more responsive and flexible to your needs.

Negotiating Improvements and Upgrades

Even in a rental, there's room to personalize and improve your living space. Here's how to approach your landlord about making changes. Present a Plan, when proposing an upgrade, come prepared with a clear plan and, if possible, cost estimates. Highlight how the improvement will benefit the property in the long run. Offer to share costs for larger improvements, consider offering to cover part of the costs or increase your rent slightly to offset the expenses. This shows commitment and can make your proposal more appealing. Highlight Long-Term Value, emphasize how the upgrade adds value to the property and could make it more attractive to future tenants. This can be a strong motivator for your landlord to agree. Successful negotiations for improvements hinge on clear communication, demonstrating the value of the proposed changes, and sometimes, a willingness to contribute financially.

Long-Term Tenancy Benefits

Being a long-term tenant comes with perks that can be leveraged for mutual benefit. Here's how your status can play to your advantage. Leverage for Negotiations, your proven track record as a reliable tenant puts you in a stronger position to negotiate terms, whether it's renewing your lease at a favorable rate or requesting upgrades. Stability for the Landlord, landlords appreciate the stability that long-term tenants provide. Highlight this as a benefit when discussing lease terms or proposing changes. Familiarity with the Property, your deep knowledge of the property makes you an asset. You can quickly identify and address maintenance issues before they escalate, saving your landlord time and money.

Embracing your role as a long-term tenant offers a foundation for negotiating improvements and fostering a positive, ongoing relationship with your landlord. In every interaction with your landlord, remember that empathy, clear communication, and a bit of strategic negotiation can go a long way. These strategies not only improve your living conditions but also contribute to a harmonious and mutually beneficial relationship. This approach, focusing on cooperation and understanding, ensures your rental feels more like a true home, where both tenant and landlord interests are aligned and respected.

5.4 Rent-to-Own Properties

A Stepping Stone to Homeownership

Navigating the path to owning a home often appears daunting for many, especially for those not yet ready to dive into the traditional housing market. However, an alternative route, the rent-to-own agreement, offers a bridge between renting and buying, providing a unique opportunity to ease into homeownership. This section will explore the structure of these agreements, how to critically assess their value, the steps involved in the process, and the potential hurdles you might encounter along the way.

Rent-to-Own Basics

At its core, a rent-to-own agreement blends the aspects of leasing and purchasing a home into one. These deals come in two main types: lease-option and lease-purchase agreements. Under a lease-option, you rent the property and retain the choice to buy it at a predetermined price before the lease expires, without being obligated to do so. The lease-purchase agreement, however, commits you to buying the property at the end of the lease term. Both arrangements typically involve paying a higher-than-market rent, with a portion of these payments going towards the down payment of the home should you decide to buy it.

Evaluating a Rent-to-Own Deal

To decide if a rent-to-own opportunity aligns with your goals, consider several critical factors. Price Evaluation, ensure the purchase price agreed upon reflects a fair market value forecasted for the future. This requires some research into the housing market trends in the area. Rent Premiums, understand exactly how much of your rent goes toward the future purchase of the home. It's crucial these terms are clear and that the arrangement makes financial sense in the context of your long-term goals. Contract Clarity, every detail, from maintenance responsibilities to price adjustments, should be explicitly outlined in the agreement to avoid future disputes or misunderstandings. Exit Strategies, particularly with lease-option agreements, you should have a clear path to walk away if you decide not to purchase, without facing excessive penalties.

Navigating the Process

Stepping into a rent-to-own agreement requires careful planning and negotiation. Here's how to navigate this process successfully. Financial Preparation, before entering an agreement, ensure your financial house is in order. This means improving your credit score, saving for a down payment beyond the rent premiums, and securing a stable income. Professional Guidance, consulting with a real estate attorney or a trusted agent experienced in rent-to-own arrangements can provide invaluable insights and guidance. They can help review the contract, negotiate terms, and plan for the purchase phase. Home Inspection, just as with buying a home outright, conducting a thorough home inspection before agreeing to a rent-to-own deal is vital. This step can uncover potential issues that could impact your willingness to purchase or the price you're willing to pay.

Potential Pitfalls

While rent-to-own offers a promising path to homeownership, it's not without its challenges. Being aware of these can help you avoid common pitfalls. Loss of Investment, if you opt not to buy the house or cannot secure financing at the end of the lease, you may lose the extra money paid above the rent price intended for the down payment. Locked-In Price, in a declining market, you might find yourself committed to a purchase price well above the home's market value at the time of buying. Maintenance Disputes, clarification on who is responsible for property maintenance, repairs, and improvements during the rental period is crucial. Without clear terms, you could be investing in a property you ultimately do not purchase. Contract Terms, some contracts may contain unfavorable conditions or lack flexibility, binding you to terms that are not advantageous. It's critical to scrutinize the agreement with legal help before signing.

In walking the line between tenant and future homeowner, the rent-to-own agreement offers a unique opportunity to gradually transition into owning a home. This arrangement can be especially appealing for those building their credit, saving for a down payment, or simply testing the waters of homeownership without the immediate commitment. However, it's a path that demands careful consideration, thorough planning, and a clear understanding of the terms and conditions involved. With the right approach, a rent-to-own property can indeed become the stepping stone to achieving your homeownership dreams.

5.5 Advocating for Renters' Rights: Becoming Part of the Solution

In the world of renting, knowledge is not just power—it's a form of protection and a tool for advocacy. Understanding your rights as a renter lays the groundwork for a fair and equitable living situation. It's where you begin to see beyond the confines of individual leases to the broader landscape of housing justice.

Deepening Your Knowledge of Tenants' Rights

The first step in becoming an advocate for renters' rights is to establish a solid foundation of knowledge. This involves familiarizing yourself with both the local ordinances and national laws that govern rental agreements, tenant-landlord interactions, and housing standards. Resources such as the Department of Housing and Urban Development (HUD) offer a wealth of information on federal regulations, while local housing authorities can provide insights into city or state-specific rules. Attend workshops or webinars hosted by tenant rights organizations. Read up on landmark cases or legislation that have shaped tenants' rights. Connect with local advocacy groups to learn from their experiences. This accumulation of knowledge not only empowers you in your personal renting experiences but also equips you to support others in your community.

Getting Involved in Advocacy

Once you're armed with information, the next step is to actively engage in advocacy efforts. This can take various forms, from joining existing movements to starting initiatives within your community. Joining Tenant Unions, these organizations work to protect renters' rights and can be powerful allies in addressing widespread issues. Participating in Local Housing Committees, these committees often influence local housing policies and regulations. Your involvement can ensure renters' voices are heard. Supporting Housing Rights Campaigns, whether it's through volunteering, donating, or simply spreading the word, supporting campaigns for affordable housing and tenants' rights contributes to larger change. Active participation in these groups and initiatives not only amplifies renters' concerns but also fosters a sense of community and solidarity among tenants.

Organizing and Mobilizing

For those who see unaddressed needs or want to tackle specific issues head-on, organizing community events, meetings, or even protests can be an effective way to advocate for renters' rights. Educational Events, hosting sessions to inform tenants about their rights can empower your community to stand up against unfair practices. Town Hall Meetings, facilitating discussions between renters, landlords, and local officials can foster understanding and prompt action on pressing issues. Direct Action, organizing protests or sit-ins in response to unjust policies or actions can draw public and media attention to renters' issues. The key to successful organizing is clear communication, a focused agenda, and inclusive participation. By bringing people together, you create a unified force that can push for meaningful changes.

Policy Change and Engagement

Ultimately, lasting change often requires adjustments to the legal and regulatory frameworks governing housing and renting.

Engaging with policymakers, whether through petitions, public comments, or lobbying efforts, is crucial in advocating for reforms that protect and benefit renters. Research and Proposals, gather data and draft proposals for policy changes that address specific issues, such as rent control or eviction protections. Building Coalitions, collaborating with other organizations or groups can strengthen your advocacy efforts. Public Campaigns, utilize social media, local media, and public events to raise awareness and support for your policy goals. Effective engagement with policymakers relies on presenting compelling evidence, demonstrating broad support, and maintaining persistent dialogue. It's about bridging the gap between the lived experiences of renters and the legislative process.

Through a deep understanding of renters' rights, active participation in advocacy, grassroots organizing, and engagement with policymakers, you can contribute to creating a more just and equitable housing system. This journey from knowledge to action reflects a commitment not only to your own rights as a renter but to the broader cause of housing justice.

As we transition from exploring the intricacies of renters' rights and advocacy, remember that every effort, no matter how small, contributes to the larger tapestry of change. The fight for fair and accessible housing is ongoing, and your involvement marks a step towards a future where everyone has a place to call home.

Conclusion

As we draw the curtains on this enlightening journey together, it's my sincerest hope that this book has armed you with the tools, insights, and wisdom you need to navigate the complex terrains of renting with unwavering confidence. From the very first page, our mission has been to transform the sometimes daunting prospect of renting into an empowering expedition of knowledge and self-advocacy.

Understanding your lease agreement is not just about signing a piece of paper; it's about laying the foundation for your renting journey, ensuring every term serves your best interest. This knowledge is your shield, protecting you from potential pitfalls and empowering you to negotiate terms that align with your aspirations and needs.

We've traversed the critical role of budgeting in securing that perfect rental — a sanctuary that doesn't just shelter you but also respects the boundaries of your financial health. Remember, a dream home exceeds its physical parameters; it's also one that fits snugly within your budget, leaving room for your life to grow and breathe.

Equally, we've underscored the importance of being versed in your rights and responsibilities. This understanding is the cornerstone of a harmonious renting experience, preventing disputes and fostering a relationship with your landlord built on mutual respect and understanding.

Personalizing your rental, within the lease's boundaries, transforms it from a mere space to a haven. It's about making a place resonate with your essence, turning it into a source of comfort and joy.

I've encouraged you to not only grasp the foundational knowledge shared but also to venture into more complex strategies for renting success. It's through applying these advanced tactics that you'll find yourself mastering the art of renting, turning every challenge into an opportunity for growth and every space into a reflection of your journey.

Building positive relationships with your landlord goes beyond mere pleasantries; it's about cultivating a partnership that benefits both parties, ensuring your time in any rental is as enjoyable as it is enriching.

And as we part ways, I urge you to continue your education on renters' rights and perhaps even engage in advocacy. The landscape of renting is ever-evolving, and staying informed is key to not only protecting your interests but also contributing to the broader fight for fair and just renting practices.

Keep this book close, not just as a token of our journey together but as a companion in all your future renting endeavors. Whether you're about to sign a new lease, negotiate your rent, or face challenges as a tenant, let this book be your guide, your reference, and your friend.

Thank you for embarking on this comprehensive exploration of renting with me. My hope is that the insights shared will serve you well, illuminating your path to renting success. As you move forward, armed with knowledge and a proactive attitude, remember that you are now well-equipped to make informed decisions in the rental market. Approach each step with confidence, knowing that you have the power to shape your renting experience into one that not only meets but exceeds your expectations.

In the spirit of empowerment and success, I wish you all the best in your renting adventures. May your journey be filled with fair leases, respectful landlord-tenant relationships, and spaces that feel unequivocally like home. Go forth with assurance, for you are no longer just a tenant in the vast world of rentals; you are a knowledgeable, empowered, and proactive member of the renting community.

Affectionately,

L.T. Judd

References

Tenants / U.S. Department of Housing and Urban Development ...

https://www.hud.gov/groups/tenants

12 tips for negotiating a commercial lease

https://www.bdc.ca/en/articles-tools/money-finance/buy-lease-commercial-real-estate/how-to-negotiate-commercial-lease-effectively

Top 10 Mistakes to Avoid in Lease Agreements - LinkedIn

https://www.linkedin.com/pulse/top-10-mistakes-avoid-lease-agreements-comprehensive-guide

How to Break a Lease Without a Penalty - Apartment List

https://www.apartmentlist.com/renter-life/break-a-lease-withou t-a-penalty

7 steps to creating a realistic budget as a renter + Rental budget calculator

https://www.thezebra.com/resources/home/creating-a-realistic -budget-as-a-renter-calculator/

Monthly Utility Costs In The US By State

https://www.forbes.com/home-improvement/living/monthly-ut ility-costs-by-state/

The Best Budget Apps for 2024

https://www.nerdwallet.com/article/finance/best-budget-apps

How to negotiate for cheaper rent

https://www.cnbc.com/2023/05/25/how-to-negotiate-for-cheap er-rent.html

Tenant Rights | HUD.gov / U.S. Department of Housing and ...

https://www.hud.gov/topics/rental_assistance/tenantrights

How to Handle Security Deposit Disputes

https://www.nolo.com/legal-encyclopedia/security-deposit-disputes

Fair Housing: Rights and Obligations - HUD

https://www.hud.gov/program_offices/fair_housing_equal_opp/fair_housing_rights_and_obligations

How Rent Withholding Works

https://www.nolo.com/legal-encyclopedia/how-rent-withholding-works.html

25+ Renter-Friendly DIYs and Decor Tips

https://abeautifulmess.com/25-decor-projects-for-renters-or-anyone/

31 Small-Space Solutions for Every Room in Your Home

https://www.bhg.com/decorating/small-spaces/strategies/space-solution-every-room/

27 Tips & Tricks for Sustainable Apartment Living

https://impactful.ninja/tips-tricks-for-sustainable-apartment-living/

7 Easy Smart Home Essentials for Renters |

Wirecutter

https://www.nytimes.com/wirecutter/blog/smart-home-essentials-renters/

Rental Market Trends in the U.S. — Price Growth Is Below ...

https://www.nerdwallet.com/article/finance/rental-market-trends

Rental Arbitrage: A Guide For Landlords and Tenants

https://www.turbotenant.com/blog/rental-arbitrage/

Tips for Negotiating Your Tenant Improvement Allowance

https://www.reoptimizer.com/real-estate-optimization-blog/tips-for-negotiating-your-tenant-improvement-allowance

Rent-To-Own Homes: How Do They Work?

https://www.ramseysolutions.com/real-estate/how-does-rent-to-own-work